श्रीमद्भगवद्गीता

पञ्चमोऽध्यायः - संन्यासयोगः

śrīmadbhagavadgītā

pañcamo'dhyāyaḥ - saṁnyāsayogaḥ

Bhagavad-Gītā Chapter Five

Sanskrit Text with Transliteration, Translation & Brief Commentary

गीता मूलं ०५

Gītā Mūlaṁ 05

गीता या मधुसूदनप्रभविणी युक्ता परं ब्रह्मणि
gītā yā madhusūdana-prabhaviṇī yuktā paraṁ brahmaṇi
या कृष्णेन कृताऽखिलं नयनवद् वक्षोऽतिगूढार्थिनी ।
yā kṛṣṇena kṛtā-'khilaṃ nayanavad vakṣo-'tigūḍhārthinī ,
या लोकत्रयस्य मार्गविधिनी धर्मस्य साक्षात्पथा
yā lokatrayasya marga-vidhinī dharmasya sākṣāt-pathā ,
सा श्रीकृष्णमुखारविन्दजनिता तस्याः मूलं प्रयच्छामि ॥
sā śrī-kṛṣṇa-mukhāravinda-janitā tasyāḥ mūlaṁ prayacchāmi .

That Gītā—which's born from Madhusūdana -- who exists in Oneness with Braham;
that Gītā—which's uttered by Krishna -- of profound visions of deep mysteries concealed within;
that Gītā—which lights the Dharma-path across the threefold world;
that Gītā—that sprung from Shri Krishna's lotus-lips
—to Her sacred roots I proceed and take refuge.

Belongs to ____________________

॥ यतो धर्मस्ततो जयः - एकं-सनातन-धर्म विजयः ॥

- yato dharmastato jayaḥ -- ekaṁ sanātana-dharma vijayaḥ -

- Where Dharma abides Victory abides -- Victory unto Ekam-Sanātana-Dharma -

I0359925

Published by: only RAMA only

Title: **Gita Mūlaṁ 05 – Bhagavad Gita Chapter Five**
Sub-Title: **Sanskrit Text with Transliteration, Translation & Brief Commentary**
A No-Opinions Commentary. Only Facts. Bhagavad-Gitā As It Truly Is.
An Excellent Resource for Sectless Gitā-Study (With Wide Margin for Taking Notes)

गीता मूलं ०५
gītā mūlaṁ 05
श्रीमद्भगवद्गीता पञ्चमोऽध्यायः - संन्यासयोगः
śrīmadbhagavadgītā pañcamo'dhyāyaḥ - saṁnyāsayogaḥ

Authors: Adarsh Saxena & Vijay Kumar

Identifiers

ISBN: 978-1-945739-75-0 (Paperback)

—o—

Coming Soon / Available:
Gita Mūlaṁ 01 – Bhagavad Gita Chapter One
Gita Mūlaṁ 02 – Bhagavad Gita Chapter Two
Gita Mūlaṁ 03 – Bhagavad Gita Chapter Three
Gita Mūlaṁ 04 – Bhagavad Gita Chapter Four
Gita Mūlaṁ 05 – Bhagavad Gita Chapter Five (Available, ISBN: 978-1-945739-75-0)
Gita Mūlaṁ 06 – Bhagavad Gita Chapter Six
Gita Mūlaṁ 07 – Bhagavad Gita Chapter Seven
Gita Mūlaṁ 08 – Bhagavad Gita Chapter Eight
Gita Mūlaṁ 09 – Bhagavad Gita Chapter Nine
Gita Mūlaṁ 10 – Bhagavad Gita Chapter Ten
Gita Mūlaṁ 11 – Bhagavad Gita Chapter Eleven
Gita Mūlaṁ 12 – Bhagavad Gita Chapter Twelve (Available, ISBN: 978-1-945739-52-1)
Gita Mūlaṁ 13 – Bhagavad Gita Chapter Thirteen
Gita Mūlaṁ 14 – Bhagavad Gita Chapter Fourteen
Gita Mūlaṁ 15 – Bhagavad Gita Chapter Fifteen (Available, ISBN: 978-1-945739-51-4)
Gita Mūlaṁ 16 – Bhagavad Gita Chapter Sixteen (Available, ISBN: 978-1-945739-76-7)
Gita Mūlaṁ 17 – Bhagavad Gita Chapter Seventeen
Gita Mūlaṁ 18 – Bhagavad Gita Chapter Eighteen
[All 18 books in this Gita Mūlaṁ series will become available by Early 2026]

—o—

Our Bhagavad-Gitā Books:
Bhagavad Gita, The Holy Book of Hindus, with Sanskrit Text, English Translation & Transliteration, No Commentary.
-ISBN: 978-1-945739-36-1 / 978-1-945739-37-8 (Paperback/Hardback. Book Size 6.14"x9.21"x190 pages)
-ISBN: 978-1-945739-39-2 (For Gitā Journaling. 8"x8"x390 pages)
-ISBN: 978-1-945739-43-9 (Convenient Pocket-Sized Edition. 4"x6"x180 pages)
-ISBN: 978-1-945739-40-8 (Legacy Book. 7.5"x9.25"x246 pages)
-ISBN: 978-1-945739-55-2 / 978-1-945739-56-9 (Paperback/Hardback. For Note-Taking. 7.5"x9.25"x190 pages)

Also Available:
- **Tulsi Ramayana—Hindu Holy Book:** Ramcharitmanas with English Translation (ISBNs: 978-1-945739-**60-6**, 978-1-945739-**61-3**)
- **Ramcharitmanas - Large/Medium/Small** (No Translation)
- **Sundarakanda:** The Fifth-Ascent of Tulsi Ramayana (ISBNs: 978-1-945739-**05-7**, 978-1-945739-**15-6**)
- **Rama Hymns:** Hanuman-Chalisa, Rāma-Raksha-Stotra, etc. (ISBNs: 978-1-945739-**25-5**, 978-1-945739-**09-5**):
- **Vivekachudamani, Fiery Crest-Jewel of Wisdom** (ISBNs: 978-1-945739-**44-6**, 978-1-945739-**45-3**, 978-1-945739-**41-5**)
- **Ashtavakra Gītā, the Fiery Octave** (ISBNs: 978-1-945739-**46-0**, 978-1-945739-**47-7**, 978-1-945739-**42-2**)
- **Legacy Books - Endowment of Devotion (several):** Journal Books of sacred Hindu Hymns around which the Holy-Name Rama Name can be written; available in Paperback and Hardcover for: **Hanuman Chalisa** (ISBN: 1945739274/ 1945739940) **Sundara-Kanda** (ISBN: 1945739908/ 1945739916) **Rama-Raksha-Stotra** (ISBN: 1945739991/ 1945739967) **Bhushundi-Ramayana** (ISBN: 1945739983/ 1945739975) **Nama-Ramayanam** (ISBN: 1945739304/ 1945739959)
- **Rama Jayam - Likhita Japam Rama-Nama Mala alongside Sacred Hindu Texts (several):** Books for writing the 'Rama' Name 100,000 Times. Rama Jayam - Likhita Japam:Rama-Nama Mala. Available in Book Size 8"x10" (Paperback) for: **Hanuman Chalisa** (ISBN: 1945739169) **Rama Raksha Stotra** (ISBN: 1945739185) **Nama-Ramayanam** (ISBN: 1945739045) **Ramashtakam** (ISBN: 1945739177) **Rama Shatanama Stotra** (ISBN: 1945739266) **Rama-Shatnamavalih** (ISBN: 1945739134) **Simple (I)** (ISBN: 1945739142)
- **Likhita Japam** - Paperback books for writing the 'Rama' Name in dotted grids: **One-Lettered Rama Mantra**, Book Size 8"x10" (ISBN: 1945739312) **Two-Lettered Rama Mantra,** Book Size 8"x10" (ISBN: 1945739320) **Three-Lettered Rama Mantra,** Book Size 8"x10" (ISBN: 1945739339) **Four-Lettered Rama Mantra,** Book Size 8"x10" (ISBN: 1945739347) **Simple (II)** Book Size 7.5"x9.25" (ISBN: 1945739193) **Simple (III)** Book Size 8"x8" (ISBN: 1945739282) **Simple (IV)** Book Size 8.5"x8.5" (ISBN: 1945739878) **Simple (V)** Book Size 8.5"x11" (ISBN: 1945739924)

CONTENTS

गीता मूलं ०५
gītā mūlaṁ 05
श्रीमद्भगवद्गीता पञ्चमोऽध्यायः - संन्यासयोगः
śrīmadbhagavadgītā pañcamo'dhyāyaḥ - saṁnyāsayogaḥ

bhagavad-gītā

श्रीमद्भगवद्गीता

प्रथमोऽध्यायः - अर्जुनविषादयोगः

धृतराष्ट्र उवाच –

धर्मक्षेत्रे कुरुक्षेत्रे समवेता युयुत्सवः ।
मामकाः पाण्डवाश्चैव किमकुर्वत सञ्जय ॥ १-१ ॥

सञ्जय उवाच –

दृष्ट्वा तु पाण्डवानीकं व्यूढं दुर्योधनस्तदा ।
आचार्यमुपसङ्गम्य राजा वचनमब्रवीत् ॥ १-२ ॥
पश्यैतां पाण्डुपुत्राणामाचार्य महतीं चमूम् ।
व्यूढां द्रुपदपुत्रेण तव शिष्येण धीमता ॥ १-३ ॥
अत्र शूरा महेष्वासा भीमार्जुनसमा युधि ।
युयुधानो विराटश्च द्रुपदश्च महारथः ॥ १-४ ॥
धृष्टकेतुश्चेकितानः काशिराजश्च वीर्यवान् ।
पुरुजित्कुन्तिभोजश्च शैब्यश्च नरपुङ्गवः ॥ १-५ ॥
युधामन्युश्च विक्रान्त उत्तमौजाश्च वीर्यवान् ।
सौभद्रो द्रौपदेयाश्च सर्व एव महारथाः ॥ १-६ ॥
अस्माकं तु विशिष्टा ये तान्निबोध द्विजोत्तम ।
नायका मम सैन्यस्य संज्ञार्थं तान्ब्रवीमि ते ॥ १-७ ॥
भवान्भीष्मश्च कर्णश्च कृपश्च समितिञ्जयः ।
अश्वत्थामा विकर्णश्च सौमदत्तिस्तथैव च ॥ १-८ ॥
अन्ये च बहवः शूरा मदर्थे त्यक्तजीविताः ।
नानाशस्त्रप्रहरणाः सर्वे युद्धविशारदाः ॥ १-९ ॥
अपर्याप्तं तदस्माकं बलं भीष्माभिरक्षितम् ।
पर्याप्तं त्विदमेतेषां बलं भीमाभिरक्षितम् ॥ १-१० ॥
अयनेषु च सर्वेषु यथाभागमवस्थिताः ।

द्वितीयोऽध्यायः - साङ्ख्ययोगः

तृतीयोऽध्यायः - कर्मयोगः

चतुर्थोऽध्यायः - ज्ञानकर्मसंन्यासयोगः

पञ्चमोऽध्यायः - संन्यासयोगः

षष्ठोऽध्यायः - ध्यानयोगः

सप्तमोऽध्यायः - ज्ञानविज्ञानयोगः

अष्टमोऽध्यायः - अक्षरब्रह्मयोगः

नवमोऽध्यायः - राजविद्याराजगुह्ययोगः

दशमोऽध्यायः - विभूतियोगः

एकादशोऽध्यायः - विश्वरूपदर्शनयोगः

द्वादशोऽध्यायः - भक्तियोगः

त्रयोदशोऽध्यायः - क्षेत्रक्षेत्रज्ञविभागयोगः

चतुर्दशोऽध्यायः - गुणत्रयविभागयोगः

पञ्चदशोऽध्यायः - पुरुषोत्तमयोगः

षोडशोऽध्यायः - दैवासुरसम्पद्विभागयोगः

सप्तदशोऽध्यायः - श्रद्धात्रयविभागयोगः

अष्टादशोऽध्यायः - मोक्षसंन्यासयोगः

ॐ ॐ ॐ ॐ ॐ ॐ ॐ ॐ ॐ ॐ ॐ ॐ ॐ ॐ ॐ ॐ ॐ ॐ

—ॐ— ध्यानम् —ॐ— dhyānam —ॐ—

—ॐ—ॐ—ॐ—ॐ—ॐ—ॐ—

ॐ INVOCATIONS

ॐ श्री परमात्मने नमः
— om śrī paramātmane namaḥ —
[Om—I bow down to the Supreme-Energy, Supreme-Being]

त्वमेव माता च पिता त्वमेव ।
tvameva mātā ca pitā tvameva ,
त्वमेव बंधुश्च सखा त्वमेव ।
tvameva baṁdhuśca sakhā tvameva ,
त्वमेव विद्या द्रविणं त्वमेव ।
tvameva vidyā draviṇaṁ tvameva ,
त्वमेव सर्वं मम देवदेव ॥
tvameva sarvaṁ mama devadeva .

Thou art my mother and my father, Thou alone my kin, kith, friend; Thou alone my wisdom, knowledge, wealth; Thou alone—O God of gods—my all, and everything!

— ॐ —

शान्ताकारं भुजगशयनं पद्मनाभं सुरेशं ।
śāntākāraṁ bhujagaśayanaṁ padmanābhaṁ sureśaṁ
विश्वाधारं गगनसदृशं मेघवर्णं शुभाङ्गम् ।
viśvādhāraṁ gaganasadṛśaṁ meghavarṇaṁ śubhāṅgam ,
लक्ष्मीकान्तं कमलनयनं योगिभिर्ध्यानगम्यं ।
lakṣmīkāntaṁ kamalanayanaṁ yogibhirdhyānagamyaṁ
वन्दे विष्णुं भवभयहरं सर्वलोकैकनाथम् ॥
vande viṣṇuṁ bhavabhayaharaṁ sarvalokaikanātham .

I venerate Shri Vishnu—of a serene appearance who slumbers upon the serpent *Shesha-Nāga*, from whose navel has sprung the lotus of creation, who presides over as the God of gods, who is the substratum of the universe, boundless and infinite like the sky. Of a dark hue like the clouds, of a form radiating everlasting auspiciousness, with eyes beautiful like lotus petals, who is the beloved of Devī Lakshmī, who is reachable only through devotional meditation by Yogīs, who removes all fears of worldly existence—upon Him, Vishnu, the One Great Lord of all the worlds, I meditate.

— ॐ —

यं ब्रह्मा वरुणेन्द्ररुद्रमरुतः स्तुन्वन्ति दिव्यैः स्तवैः
yaṁ brahmā varuṇendrarudramarutaḥ stunvanti divyaiḥ stavaiḥ
वेदैः साङ्गपदक्रमोपनिषदैर्गायन्ति यं सामगाः ।
vedaiḥ sāṅgapadakramopaniṣadairgāyanti yaṁ sāmagāḥ ,
ध्यानावस्थिततद्गतेन मनसा पश्यन्ति यं योगिनो
dhyānāvasthitatadgatena manasā paśyanti yaṁ yogino
यस्यान्तं न विदुः सुरासुरगणा देवाय तस्मै नमः ॥
yasyāntaṁ na viduḥ surāsuragaṇā devāya tasmai namaḥ .

Unto That Supreme—whom Brahammā, Varuna, Indra, Rudra and the Mārutas praise with excellent holy hymns; who is versified throughout the Vedas and Upanishads by the chanters of Sāma; who—in perfect meditations deep—the yogis see within their own minds while absorbed in "That-One"; whose beginning and end, even gods and demi-gods never know of—unto That Supreme-Being, I offer my many venerations.

ॐ ॐ ॐ ॐ ॐ ॐ ॐ ॐ ॐ ॐ ॐ ॐ ॐ ॐ ॐ ॐ ॐ ॐ

—ॐ— स्तुतिः —ॐ— stutiḥ —ॐ—

—ॐ—ॐ—ॐ—ॐ—ॐ—ॐ—

VENERATIONS

— ॐ —

पार्थाय प्रतिबोधितां भगवता नारायणेन स्वयम्
pārthāya pratibodhitāṁ bhagavatā nārāyaṇena svayam
व्यासेनग्रथितां पुराणमुनिना मध्ये महाभारते ।
vyāsenagrathitāṁ purāṇamuninā madhye mahābhārate ,
अद्वैतामृतवर्षिणीं भगवतीमष्टादशाध्यायिनीम्
advaitāmṛtavarṣiṇīṁ bhagavatīmaṣṭādaśādhyāyinīm
अम्ब त्वामनुसन्दधामि भगवद्गीते भवेद्वेषिणीम् ॥
amba tvāmanusandadhāmi bhagavadgīte bhavedveṣiṇīm .

O Thou Bhagavad-Gītā—with whom Pārtha was enlightened by the Lord Nārāyana himself; who was integrated into the Mahābhārata by the ancient sage Vyāsa; O Thou blessed Mother—who with her eighteen Cantos shower humanity with the nectar of Advaita; O Thou destroyer of rebirths, upon Thee—O Bhagavad-Gītā, O loving Mother—I meditate.

— ॐ —

नमोऽस्तु ते व्यास विशालबुद्धे फुल्लारविन्दायतपत्रनेत्र ।
namo'stu te vyāsa viśālabuddhe phullāravindāyatapatranetra ,
येन त्वया भारततैलपूर्णः प्रज्वालितो ज्ञानमयः प्रदीपः ॥
yena tvayā bhāratatailapūrṇaḥ prajvālito jñānamayaḥ pradīpaḥ .

Salutations to Thee O Vyāsa—of a mighty intellect and with eyes large like the petals of a full-blossomed lotus; by whom has been forever lit in this world the Lamp-of-Wisdom, filled with the oil in the form of the great epic: Mahābhārata.

— ॐ —

प्रपन्नपारिजाताय तोत्रवेत्रैकपाणये ।
prapannapārijātāya totravetraikapāṇaye ,
ज्ञानमुद्राय कृष्णाय गीतामृतदुहे नमः ॥
jñānamudrāya kṛṣṇāya gītāmṛtaduhe namaḥ .

He—who is the wish-granting tree of the suppliant—in whose one hand is held the rope for cow and with the other hand who holds the Yogic posture of *Jnana*—who is the milcher of the nectar known as Gītā—unto Him, Krishna, my repeated venerations.

— ॐ —

सर्वोपनिषदो गावो दोग्धा गोपालनन्दनः ।
sarvopaniṣado gāvo dogdhā gopālanandanaḥ ,
पार्थो वत्सः सुधीर्भोक्ता दुग्धं गीतामृतं महत् ॥
pārtho vatsaḥ sudhīrbhoktā dugdhaṁ gītāmṛtaṁ mahat .

All the Upanishads are the cows; the milcher is the joy of cowherds, Krishna; Pārtha is the calf; the man of purified understanding is the partaker; and the milk is verily the supreme nectar known as Gītā.

— ॐ —

वसुदेवसुतं देवं कंसचाणूरमर्दनम् ।
vasudevasutaṁ devaṁ kaṁsacāṇūramardanam ,
देवकीपरमानन्दं कृष्णं वन्दे जगद्गुरुम् ॥
devakīparamānandaṁ kṛṣṇaṁ vande jagadgurum .

I worship the charioteer, the Lord-God, the destroyer of Kamsa and Chānura, the supreme joy of Devakī, the son of Vāsudeva—Shri Krishna, Jagad-Guru.

— ॐ —

भीष्मद्रोणतटा जयद्रथजला गान्धारनीलोत्पला
bhīṣmadroṇataṭā jayadrathajalā gāndhāranīlotpalā
शल्यग्राहवती कृपेण वहनी कर्णेन वेलाकुला ।
śalyagrāhavatī kṛpeṇa vahanī karṇena velākulā ,
अश्वत्थामविकर्णघोरमकरा दुर्योधनावर्तिनी
aśvatthāmavikarṇaghoramakarā duryodhanāvartinī
सोत्तीर्णा खलु पाण्डवैरणनदी कैवर्तकः केशवः ॥
sottīrṇā khalu pāṇḍavairaṇanadī kaivartakaḥ keśavaḥ .

That terrible battle-river—which had Bhīṣma and Droṇa as its two banks, and Jayadrathaja as its waters; which had the king of Gāndhāra as its blue lotus, and Śalya as its shark; whose currents and billows were Kṛipā and Karṇa; which had Aśvatthāmā and Vikarṇa as its terrible alligators; and of which Duryodhana was the deadly whirlpool—that ferocious river could be forded by the Pāṇḍavas only because they had Keśava as their helmsman.

— ॐ —

पाराशर्यवचः सरोजममलं गीतार्थगन्धोत्कटं
pārāśaryavacaḥ sarojamamalaṁ gītārthagandhotkaṭaṁ
नानाख्यानककेसरं हरिकथासम्बोधनाबोधितम्।
nānākhyānakakesaraṁ harikathāsambodhanābodhitam ।
लोके सज्जनषट्पदैरहरहः पेपीयमानं मुदा
loke sajjanaṣaṭpadairaharahaḥ pepīyamānaṁ mudā
भूयाद्भारतपङ्कजं कलिमलप्रध्वंसिनः श्रेयसे ॥
bhūyādbhāratapaṅkajaṁ kalimalapradhvaṁsinaḥ śreyase .

May this Lotus called Mahābhārata—which was born on the lake of the words of Vyāsa—which is perfumed with the fragrance of the Purport-of-Gītā—which has its innumerous stories as the pollen—which became fully bloomed through the discourses of Hari—which is the destroyer of the sins of the Kali-Yuga—which is everyday partaken joyously by the bees in the shape of good people of the world—may it bestow all goodness upon us.

— ॐ —

मूकं करोति वाचालं पङ्गुं लङ्घयते गिरिम् ।
mūkaṁ karoti vācālaṁ paṅguṁ laṅghayate girim ,
यत्कृपा तमहं वन्दे परमानन्दमाधवम् ॥
yatkṛpā tamahaṁ vande paramānandamādhavam .

I salute the Supreme-Being of the nature of supreme bliss, by whose very grace the dumb become eloquent and the cripples step across mountains.

— ॐ —

ॐ पूर्णमदः पूर्णमिदं पूर्णात् पूर्णमुदच्यते ।
om pūrṇamadaḥ pūrṇamidaṁ pūrṇāt pūrṇamudacyate ,
पूर्णस्य पूर्णमादाय पूर्णमेवावशिष्यते ।
pūrṇasya pūrṇamādāya pūrṇamevāvaśiṣyate ,
ॐ शान्तिः शान्तिः शान्तिः ॥
om śāntiḥ śāntiḥ śāntiḥ .

Om—That One (the unmanifest Brahma)—is infinite, complete, Entire; this (the manifest universe) is entire; And from That One fullness has emerged this entire universe here; And even when this entirety here is taken out of that One-Entire, It still abides complete in all Its entireness! Om, peace—let there be tranquility all around me!

— ॐ — ॐ — ॐ — ॐ — ॐ — ॐ — ॐ — ॐ — ॐ —

ॐ THE JOURNEY THUS FAR

— ॐ तत सत ॐ —

The Bhagavad-Gītā, the Divine Song of Bhagwāna Shri Krishna is a timeless revelation of truth—a dialogue not merely between a prince on a battlefield and his charioteer, but between the perplexed human soul and the Eternal Divine. Set upon the sacred terrain of Kurukshetra, it does not just recount the tale of warriors and their wars but unveils the profound within-war that's taking place all around: the struggle between dharma and adharma -- righteousness and unrighteousness, between the fleeting and the eternal, between the self bound by illusion and the Self radiant in the fiery wisdom of Sanātana-Dharma.

The Gītā is no ordinary scripture. It is the song of life sung by the Supreme-Being Himself—Bhagwāna Shri Krishna—unto the anguished Arjuna who stands at the cusp of a duty too great to bear and a wisdom too deep to ignore. The Gitā is a light for all ages—especially for all who seek clarity amidst chaos, strength amidst despair, and freedom amid bondage.

THE JOURNEY THUS FAR: FROM DESPONDENCY TO DISCERNMENT

The Gitā journey begins at **Chapter 1 – Arjuna Viṣāda Yoga,** where the mighty warrior Arjuna, beholding his own kith and kin arrayed before him, is overtaken by sorrow and confusion. His limbs falter, his bow slips from his hand, and his will to fight vanishes. He sees not victory nor joy in slaying his own, and thus lays down his weapons, seeking refuge in despair. This chapter sets the stage—not of external war alone—but of the soul's inner crisis, when dharma becomes obscured and the heart trembles.

In Chapter 2 – Sāṅkhya Yoga, the Lord begins His sublime instruction. Krishna imparts the eternal wisdom of the Ātmā—our indestructible Self that stays untouched by death or change. He introduces the twin paths of knowledge (jñāna) and action (karma), urging Arjuna to rise above attachment and perform his duties with equanimity. This chapter is a vast ocean of philosophical depth, outlining the vision of reality as seen by the wise.

Chapter 3 – Karma Yoga unfolds the nobility of performing karmas for dharma's sake, without selfish desires. Here, Shri Krishna expounds the glory of niṣkāma karma—action without attachment to results—as a sacred offering unto the Divine. The Jiva is not to abandon action but to sanctify it—to transform daily work into a path to liberation. By fulfilling one's svadharma without ego, one rises above bondages.

Chapter 4 – Jñāna-Karma-Saṃnyāsa Yoga reveals a deeper dimension—how true knowledge illuminates action. The Lord declares the ancient lineage of this teaching and speaks of His own divine incarnations undertaken to uphold Sanātana-Dharma. He unveils the secret of karma-yoga—karma performed purified by jñāna, with all bondages of actions burned away in the fire of knowledge. It is not mere renunciation of deeds, but renunciation of the sense of doership that leads to emancipation.

Now with this book, we arrive at the threshold of **Chapter 5 – Karma-Saṃnyāsa Yoga,** where the subtle distinction between renunciation (saṃnyāsa) and the yoga of action (karma-yoga) is further clarified. Arjuna, still seeking to reconcile these paths, is guided by the Lord to perceive their underlying unity. True renunciation is not in the outward abandonment of work, but in the inner relinquishment of craving and ego. The illumined person sees inaction in action and action in inaction, and thus knowing the essence of karma, remains ever free.

GLIMPSES OF WHAT LIES AHEAD

As the Gītā unfolds beyond this juncture, the teachings ascend in both subtlety and splendour. **Chapter 6** deepens the path of meditation **(Dhyāna-yoga)**, leading the soul inward to commune with the Self.

Chapters 7 to 12 will unveil the Lord's divine nature, both immanent and transcendent—culminating in the awe-inspiring vision of the Viśvarūpa, the cosmic form. The seeker is drawn into the mystery of bhakti, devotion that bridges the finite and the Infinite.

Chapters 13 to 18 of the Bhagavad-Gitā bring the teaching to its full flowering, as the Lord illumines the field and the knower of the field, the guṇas that bind, and the paths of liberation. All culminates in the supreme teaching of surrender—'sarva-dharmān parityajya māṁ ekaṁ śaraṇaṁ vraja'—where the soul is called to take full refuge in the Lord and His Dharma.

The Bhagavad-Gītā is not merely a dialogue; it is a pilgrimage of the soul. From the darkness of confusion to the dawn of Self-knowledge, from bondage to freedom, from fear to the fearless embrace of Truth—this is the path the Gītā reveals. And as we stand at the opening of Chapter 5, we do so with reverence, ready to enter deeper into the sacred mystery of renunciation and action, of wisdom and surrender, of man and the Divine—and of man eventually becoming Divine himself.

— ॐ श्रीनिवासाय नमः ॐ —

Gita, a Voice from God to Man—As if from Friend to Friend

O Gita, from lips of God to warrior's ear, Thy teaching gently pour,
Like a father speaks, or a comrade true—or Sovereign without a sword.
Though Arjuna's bow was cast aside, And fear had veiled his sight,
Thou didst arise, O Gita bright,
To decimate doubts — Fill mind with light.

Across the veils of endless Time, thou singest still, serene & clear—
To hearts that falter in the dusk—to souls who thirst, to those who fear.
Across generations, thou speakest still, to each whose heart has strayed,
Who stands in life's bewildering field—unsure, alone, afraid.
When sureness dances lost in mist,
And arrows fly through inner skies,
Thy song, O Gita, silvers forth—moonbeams bright, where grimness lies.

O seeker, hark! this Hymn is thine—which once was voiced in Arjun's ear,
Its fire thaws the wintered heart, and draw one to a star-lit sphere.
Thou too shalt rise in wisdom armed—when Truth's low thunder stirs the sky,
And stride the path few mortals tread, standing neath gaze of Rishis nigh.

And Then solo thou shalt ascend
—unaccompanied yes, but not lonesome—
For thou shalt have become the Ocean itself—
Become the entire Cosmos... each everyone and each everything..
Thy True Self, long veiled, will have awakened,
Thy Divinity arisen,
—And—
Manifesting the Mantra अहं ब्रह्मास्मि Aham-Braham-Asmi,
A blazing god shalt ascend on high,
Unveiled beneath eternal skies.

ॐ CHAPTER FIVE, A BIRD'S-EYE VIEW

— ॐ तत सत ॐ —

KARMA-SAṀNYĀSA YOGA: THE HARMONY OF RENUNCIATION AND ACTION

As the sacred dialogue of the Bhagavad-Gītā advances, Chapter Five stands as a radiant threshold—where the seeming duality between saṁnyāsa (renunciation) and karma-yoga (selfless action) is resolved with luminous clarity.

This is a chapter of harmonization, not of opposition; here we glean the revelation that the outward form of our path is secondary to our inner disposition. Here Bhagwāna Shri Krishna, the Supreme Teacher, draws together the strands of Jnāna and Karma—and of renunciation and engagement, and of deep tranquility and intense service—weaving them into a unified vision of spiritual perfection.

Arjuna, still confused about the difference between physically renouncing the world versus living within it performing work without attachments, poses a question born of sincere inquiry. Shri Krishna answers not with dry distinctions, but with deep insight, revealing that both paths, rightly followed, lead to liberation—except that the path of action, performed with detachment, is found to be in many ways superior and more accessible.

This chapter is a hymn to the sthita-prajña, the sage of stable wisdom—who, though acting in the world, remains untouched by it. It extols the serene joy born of inner detachment, the unwavering equality of vision that sees the Divine in all, and the quiet bliss of one who, having transcended the pairs of opposites, abides ever in the Self.

CHAPTER FIVE: A VERSE-BY-VERSE OVERVIEW

Now let us move through the sacred terrain of this profound chapter verse by verse, beholding the spiritual architecture it unfolds.

Verse 1

Arjuna inquires: Which is better—renunciation of action, or selfless action? His question reflects the heart of many seekers who stay caught between the impulse to withdraw and the call to serve.

Verses 2–6

Shri Krishna gently but firmly resolves the doubt: Both lead to the highest good, but karma-yoga—the path of performing one's ordained duty—is superior for most, as it neither forsakes duty nor fosters aversion. The true renunciate is he who acts without desire, not merely he who renounces outer work. In truth, the one established in karma-yoga is already a saṁnyāsī, free from duality and full of equanimity.

Verses 7–10

The Lord paints the portrait of the illumined one: pure in heart, self-controlled, and serene. Such a soul, acting in the world without attachment, remains untouched—like the lotus leaf on water. He sees himself not as the doer; all action flows through him as a river through its course, while he remains anchored in the Self.

Verses 11–12

These verses contrast the wise, who offer all actions to the Divine and attain peace, with the unwise, who act with ego and become bound. True peace comes not necessarily from passivity, but it is a state of mind.

Verses 13–14

The enlightened one, having abandoned the sense of agency, rests in inner stillness. Though the body may move about performing work, he knows the Self does not act. Action belongs to nature (prakṛti), not to the Self—who remains ever untouched.

Verse 15

Here, Krishna refutes the notion that the Divine causes suffering or evil. It is the veil of ignorance that clouds human vision. The Supreme neither favours nor condemns, but shines impartially like the sun.

Verses 16–17

For those whose ignorance is dispelled by knowledge, the Self is revealed like the rising sun dispels night. Such souls are fixed in the Supreme, their minds absorbed in the Eternal, their lives offered in wisdom.

Verses 18–19

The mark of such wisdom is samatva—equality. The sage sees a brāhmaṇa, a cow, an elephant, a dog, and dog-eater with the same vision—recognising the Divine essence in all. For one established in this equality, rebirth holds no bondage.

Verse 20

Unshaken by pleasure or pain, gain or loss, the knower of Braham abides content, undisturbed, rooted in the unchanging Self.

Verses 21–23

True joy is not in the external but within. The wise renounce sense-pleasures, knowing their fleeting nature and hidden sorrow. He who can endure the urges of desire and anger even here, in the body, is a true yogin and finds peace.

Verse 24

The inner light shines in the one whose happiness is within, whose delight is in the Self, and whose vision is turned inward. Such a being becomes liberated in this very life.

Verses 25-26

The seers who are free of desire and anger, their minds purified by knowledge and discipline, attain the bliss of union with Braham—a Supreme Peace like no other.

Verses 27-28

A glimpse is given of the yogin's inward discipline: control of the senses, regulated breath, withdrawal of attention from the outer world, and the steady contemplation of the Divine. Through such inwardness, he is released from fear and attains the silence of the Self.

Verse 29

The chapter concludes with a profound proclamation: The Lord is the partaker of all Yajnas, the Master of all worlds, and the well-wisher of all beings. Knowing Him thus, the soul attains lasting peace.

— ॐ —

Canto-Five stands as a bridge—a bridge between renunciation and action, between wisdom and devotion, between the outer world and the inner Self. It reveals that true renunciation is not a matter of place, robe, or occupation—but a matter of freedom from cravings, a mind anchored in equanimity, and a heart surrendered to the Lord.

Now Let us proceed with the study of this Canto with deep reverence. Let us perceive the harmony of life and liberation, of stillness in action, and of silence in speech. By the time we reach its end, Canto-Five shall have prepared us for an ascent into deeper stillness still—into the path of meditation -- which shall be unveiled in Canto-Six.

ॐ ॐ ॐ ॐ ॐ ॐ ॐ ॐ ॐ ॐ ॐ ॐ ॐ ॐ ॐ ॐ ॐ ॐ

पञ्चमोऽध्यायः - संन्यासयोगः
pañcamo'dhyāyaḥ - saṁnyāsayogaḥ
:: Canto – V ::
- Renunciation of Action –

ॐ ॐ ॐ ॐ ॐ ॐ ॐ ॐ ॐ ॐ ॐ ॐ ॐ ॐ ॐ ॐ ॐ ॐ

ॐ गीता श्लोकः ५.१ – Gītā Verse 5.1

ॐ श्रीमद्भगवद्गीतासूपनिषत्सु ब्रह्मविद्यायां योगशास्त्रे श्रीकृष्णार्जुनसंवादे
om śrīmadbhagavadgītāsūpaniṣatsu brahmavidyāyāṁ yogaśāstre śrīkṛṣṇārjunasaṁvāde
संन्यासयोगो नाम पञ्चमोऽध्यायः श्लोकः १
saṁnyāsayogo nāma pañcamo'dhyāyaḥ ślokaḥ 1

— ॐ —

अर्जुन उवाच --
arjuna uvāca --

संन्यासं कर्मणां कृष्ण पुनर्योगं च शंससि ।
saṁnyāsaṁ karmaṇāṁ kṛṣṇa punaryogaṁ ca śaṁsasi
यच्छ्रेय एतयोरेकं तन्मे ब्रूहि सुनिश्चितम् ॥५-१॥
yacchreya etayorekaṁ tanme brūhi suniścitam (5-1)

***Arjuna said:* "O Krishna, on the one hand you extol renunciation of action, but then again you exhort me towards action as well; pray tell me decidedly the one thing which is conducive to my good."** (5.1)

—: Word-by-Word :—

अर्जुन उवाच arjuna uvāca – Arjuna said; संन्यासम् saṁnyāsaṁ – renunciation; कर्मणाम् karmaṇāṁ – of actions; कृष्ण kṛṣṇa – O Krishna; पुनः punaḥ – again; योगम् yogaṁ – the path of yoga; च ca – and; शंससि śaṁsasi – you praise; यत् yat – which; श्रेयो śreya – is better; एतयोः etayoḥ – of these two; एकम् ekam – one; तन्मे tanme – that to me; ब्रूहि brūhi – please tell; सुनिश्चितम् suniścitam – with certainty.

—: Understanding The Verse :—

— ॐ श्रीकृष्णाय नमः ॐ —

"O Charioteer, whose every word awakens a new Dawn,
Thou speak'st of tranquil stillness, yet summon me to war anon!
Here I stand—a place where mercy & dharma have become intertwined,
Between arrows-of-steel and blanket mercy, I see no path for me well defined.

Betwixt blades of swords and turning away in retreat,
which path is better, do tell me, please.

O, why canst I cast off these horrendous duties,
Throw karmas to the wind—just walk away free?
Must I have to wear these karmas as my brace?
Ah, it will be so simple—to shrug away these duties, these karmas,
—And vanish without a trace!

Ah me, the heart of mine drifts in fate's vast abyss,
Yearning after God, who stays veiled behind that and this.
I keep questioning Him.
But I will not stop till an answer is found—yes, I will keep at it."

Aye, O Mortal,
Only through such questioning—persistent, brave, deep,
the soul stirs from all slumbers—refusing to die in stuporous sleep.

— ॐ श्रीकृष्णाय नमः ॐ —

In this verse, the noble Arjuna, still grappling with inner conflict, turns once again to Bhagavān Shri Krishna, whom he addresses directly by name.

Arjuna seeks clarity between the paths of renunciation संन्यास (sannyāsa) and karma कर्म योग (karma yoga), unsure which leads more surely to liberation. His appeal reflects a deep yearning for resolution—not only in doctrine but within his own unsettled mind.

Arjuna's continued questioning reveals his trust in Krishna as the supreme guide who can illuminate the way through the dilemmas of dharma.

— ॐ श्रीरामाय नमः ॐ —

Arjuna voices a fundamental spiritual quandary. Throughout the preceding discourses, he has heard Shri Krishna speak in praise of both संन्यास Sannyāsa — the renunciation of action — and also कर्म योग Karma-Yoga — the performance of action without attachment to its fruits.

To Arjuna, these two paths appear divergent, even contradictory. Arjuna isn't merely requesting an intellectual clarification, but is sincerely yearning to discern the one path that is most श्रेय śreyas — truly auspicious and conducive to the highest good.

And what is Jiva's highest good?

It is, liberation मोक्ष (mokṣa)—emancipation from this sorrowful transmigratory cycle of births and deaths in which we have stayed revolving for eons now!

Arjuna's question is not idle curiosity, but a cry for spiritual clarity amidst the ambiguities of life, dharma, duty.

— ॐ अजाय नमः ॐ —

This verse thus marks a pivotal moment: Arjuna seeks not abstract knowledge but a decisive guidance on how to live a life of inner freedom amidst outer action—a life that doesn't further entangle one within the world but truly emancipates.

The confusion Arjuna voices mirrors is the age-old tension between contemplative life and active life — a tension that the Gītā seeks to reconcile through its sublime doctrine of Yogayukta Karma.

—: Key Sanskrit Terms :—

The words here are like two lamps set side by side, one burning with renunciation, the other with action. Arjuna's voice wavers between them, asking which is higher. Let us look closely at the key Sanskrit terms, allowing their rich connotations to shed light on deeper dimensions. Each syllable glows with tension, a yearning for resolution in the flicker of flame.

— ॐ —

संन्यासं (Saṁnyāsaṁ):

Saṁnyāsa here signifies not merely the outer renunciation of works, but the inward laying down of all clinging to action and its fruits.

It is the sacred act of placing all deeds at the altar of the Eternal, renouncing the sense of कृतत्व kartṛtva (doership) itself.

In Arjuna's query, संन्यास saṁnyāsa carries both the fragrance of complete inward withdrawal and the life of the renunciate who has transcended the binding forces of karma.

— ॐ —

कर्मणां (Karmaṇāṁ):

Karmaṇāṁ points specifically to the actions prescribed by the Vedic ordinances — duties born of one's station वर्ण (varṇa) and stage of life आश्रम (āśrama).

Beyond the outer ritual, this word also hints at the inevitable movement of प्रकिति prakṛti (Nature) and the participation of the embodied soul within the dance of having become embodied.

Alas, now that this body stays donned upon us, we have to take care of its endless wants!

But mind it, the wants of this body may be endless but not all are legit—only those, which have the sanction of सनातनधर्म Sanātana-Dharma, the cosmic law, are.

— ॐ —

योगं (Yogaṁ):

Here yoga is not a mere mechanical discipline, but the art of कर्म-योग karma-yoga — the sacred synthesis wherein action is performed without desire for its fruit—instead consecrated to the Supreme.

योग Yoga unites action and renunciation inwardly, harmonizing the realm of change संसार (saṁsāra) with the changeless Self आत्मा (Ātmā).

— ॐ —

श्रेयः (Śreyaḥ):

श्रेयः Śreyaḥ is that which leads to the highest good — the eternal welfare of the soul, distinct from प्रेय preyas, the fleeting satisfaction of worldly desires.

Arjuna seeks that which does not merely console the mind, but elevates the spirit beyond death—takes it beyond all wants!

— ॐ —

सुनिश्चितम् (Suniścitam):

सुनिश्चितम् Suniścitam conveys a finality of discernment, an unerring decision free from doubt संषय (saṁśaya).

Arjuna, tossed between apparent contradictions, craves from Krishna a definitive guidance — a teaching not colored by circumstance, but rooted in eternal truth.

See how each word of Arjuna's prayer weaves a tapestry of the soul's yearning for certitude amidst the bewildering interplay of renunciation and engagement.

—: *In Brief* :—

— ॐ श्रीकृष्णाय नमः ॐ —

Here, Arjuna addresses the Supreme Lord as कृष्ण Krishna, whose name, derived from the root कृ kṛṣ (to draw), signifies "He who draws all beings unto Himself through divine bliss."

The suffix ण ṇa connotes eternal joy — thus, कृष्ण Krishna is the embodiment of attraction born of blissful divinity.

By invoking this sacred name, Arjuna acknowledges Shri Krishna as both the all-knowing guide and the inward-dwelling Lord capable of dispelling his doubt from its very root.

— ॐ श्रीरामाय नमः ॐ —

Although at first glance, Arjuna's question may appear to be a repetition of his earlier inquiry in Chapter 3, but there is now a deeper evolution in his understanding.

There, Arjuna questioned why he was being urged into battle if wisdom was superior to action. Here, the inquiry is subtler. Having listened to the Lord's exaltation of ज्ञानयोग Jnānayajña (the Yajña of Knowledge) in Chapter 4, as well as the path of the path of performing one's ordained dharma through कर्मयोग Karma-Yoga, Arjuna is now faced with the seeming duality: renunciation vs. action.

If renunciation leads to liberation, then why engage in worldly activity? And if action is to be performed, then what becomes of renunciation?

— ॐ महाधनुष्मते नमः ॐ —

Beyond the fog of confusion, remember: the Gītā never extols mere renunciation of action as supreme. What Shri Krishna discards is not action itself, but the egoistic notion of doership and desire for fruits.

In Chapter 4, the Lord expounded that all actions, when performed in the spirit of यज्ञ Yajña — as an offering to the Divine — become instruments of purification and transcendence.

Thus, true renunciation is the inner state of one who, even while acting, remains unattached — संन्यास Sannyāsa in its highest form is not abandonment of action, but renunciation of the sense of proprietorship and craving.

— ॐ मायामानुष चरित्राय नमः ॐ —

Arjuna's perplexity arises from perceiving संन्यास Sannyāsa and कर्मयोग Karma-Yoga as mutually exclusive. But Bhagwāna Shri Krishna sees through the illusion of this opposition.

In His divine teaching, Shri Krishna will now proceed to unfold that these two are not separate paths but convergent ones, provided they are rightly understood.

Remember: when action is suffused with wisdom and detachment, कर्मयोग Karma-Yoga itself becomes the highest renunciation.

— ॐ स्मितवक्त्राय नमः ॐ —

Arjuna's question, though prompted by apparent contradiction, serves as a gateway for Shri Krishna to illumine the profound unity between ज्ञानयोग Jnāna-yoga and कर्मयोग Karma-yoga, leading to the supreme goal — liberation while still living जीवनमुक्ति (jīvanmukti).

The next verse thus commences the Lord's decisive resolution of this dilemma, wherein He will reveal the deeper harmony between wisdom and action — a synthesis that lies at the very heart of the Bhagavad-Gītā's eternal message.

— ॐ तत सत ॐ —

Before we move on, let us bow in reverence to this sacred verse. Write it by hand, reflect on its meaning, chant it aloud, make it your own.

— ॐ —

अर्जुन उवाच–
arjuna uvāca –
संन्यासं कर्मणां कृष्ण पुनर्योगं च शंससि ।
saṁnyāsaṁ karmaṇāṁ kṛṣṇa punaryogaṁ ca śaṁsasi
यच्छ्रेय एतयोरेकं तन्मे ब्रूहि सुनिश्चितम् ॥५-१॥
yacchreya etayorekaṁ tanme brūhi suniścitam (5-1)

ॐ

अर्जुन उवाच -- arjuna uvāca –
संन्यासं कर्मणां कृष्ण पुनर्योगं च शंससि ।
saṁnyāsaṁ karmaṇāṁ kṛṣṇa punaryogaṁ ca śaṁsasi
यच्छ्रेय एतयोरेकं तन्मे ब्रूहि सुनिश्चितम् ॥५-१॥
yacchreya etayorekaṁ tanme brūhi suniścitam (5-1)

ॐ तत्सदिति श्रीमद्भगवद्गीतासूपनिषत्सु ब्रह्मविद्यायां योगशास्त्रे श्रीकृष्णार्जुनसंवादे
om tatsaditi śrīmadbhagavadgītāsūpaniṣatsu brahmavidyāyāṁ yogaśāstre śrīkṛṣṇārjunasaṁvāde
संन्यासयोगो नाम पञ्चमोऽध्यायः श्लोकः १
saṁnyāsayogo nāma pañcamo'dhyāyaḥ ślokaḥ 1

Om-Tat-Sat—Om (Braham) is the sole Reality. In the Yogic Scripture on the Science-of-Braham, the Shrimada-Bhāgvada-Gītā Upanishad, we hereby conclude Shloka 1 of the Dialogue between Shrī Krishna and Arjuna entitled Sanyāsa-Yoga, Canto V.

— ॐ श्रीकृष्णगोविंदाय नमः ॐ —

<u>The Yogi</u>

He no longer wants—nay, not even joy.
No longer he fears—nay, not even the body's loss.
The twin fires—ire and desire—didst flicker in his past
Now only ashes whisper—the embers lost in silence.
The mind, once storm and thunder, has entered a holy stillness
like breath exhaled vanishing into sky infinite.
No stirring. No seeking.. Nary no longing.
His life is just a continuing breathing within Sanatana-Dharma.

ॐ गीता श्लोकः ५.२ – Gītā Verse 5.2

ॐ श्रीमद्भगवद्गीतासूपनिषत्सु ब्रह्मविद्यायां योगशास्त्रे श्रीकृष्णार्जुनसंवादे
om śrīmadbhagavadgītāsūpaniṣatsu brahmavidyāyāṁ yogaśāstre śrīkṛṣṇārjunasaṁvāde
संन्यासयोगो नाम पञ्चमोऽध्यायः श्लोकः २
saṁnyāsayogo nāma pañcamo'dhyāyaḥ ślokaḥ 2

— ॐ —

श्रीभगवानुवाच -- śrībhagavānuvāca --

संन्यासः कर्मयोगश्च निःश्रेयसकरावुभौ ।
saṁnyāsaḥ karmayogaśca niḥśreyasakarāvubhau
तयोस्तु कर्मसंन्यासात्कर्मयोगो विशिष्यते ॥५-२॥
tayostu karmasaṁnyāsātkarmayogo viśiṣyate (5-2)

***Shri Bhagwāna said:* "Sanyāsa—the complete renunciation of action; and Karma-Yoga—the physical performance of duty but renouncing it mentally: they are both good and lead to emancipation. Of the two however, the path of Karma-Yoga—being easier to practice—is deemed superior.** (5.2)

—: Word-by-Word :—

श्रीभगवानुवाच śrībhagavān uvāca – the Blessed Lord said; संन्यासः saṁnyāsaḥ – renunciation; कर्मयोगः karma-yogaḥ – and the path of performing ordained karma; च ca – and; निःश्रेयसकरौ niḥśreyasa-karaubhau – both lead to the highest good; तयोः tayostu – of these two; कर्मसंन्यासात karma-saṁnyāsāt – from renunciation of action; कर्मयोगः karma-yogaḥ – the path of performing ordained karma; विशिष्यते viśiṣyate – is superior.

—: Understanding The Verse :—

— ॐ श्रीकृष्णाय नमः ॐ —

In this verse, Bhagwāna Shri Krishna graciously responds to Arjuna's earnest inquiry by placing before him the essential harmony and hierarchy of two great spiritual paths: Sannyāsa, the path of renunciation, and Karma-Yoga, the path of action performed without attachment.

Both paths, Krishna declares, are efficacious in leading the aspirant toward the supreme goal of मोक्ष mokṣa, or spiritual liberation; and yet, among the two, कर्म-योग Karma-Yoga is stated to be superior—not in metaphysical potency, but in accessibility and suitability for practice, particularly for one who must still stay immersed in worldly duties and identifications – for he is yet so far away from the सन्यास-आश्रम sanyāsa-āshram that comes only in the fourth quarter of life.

— ॐ श्रीरामाय नमः ॐ —

This teaching underscores a recurring principle in the Gītā: the path of inner renunciation amidst outer action is more fruitful than premature withdrawal from life.

The Lord, ever compassionate and discerning of each soul's constitution, elaborates why the Yoga of performing ordained karma is not only a preparatory ground for higher knowledge but also a complete path in itself.

—: Key Sanskrit Terms :—

Let us pause to consider the verse's principal Sanskrit expressions, each of which serves as a gateway to the verse's deeper philosophical currents. Let us rest with the verse as with a teacher weighing gold on scales. Renunciation and yoga of action are both noble, yet action done without clinging is higher. Each word tips the balance gently, clarifying without dismissing.

— ॐ —

संन्यासः (Saṁnyāsaḥ):

Here **संन्यासः** saṁnyāsaḥ evokes the sacred renunciation wherein the seeker abandons all karmic actions, both external and internal, seeing no further necessity for acts born of desire or duty.

It isn't mere physical withdrawal but an inner severance from the wheel of karma, rooted in the full knowledge of the Self as actionless.

— ॐ —

कर्मयोगः (Karma-yogaḥ):

कर्मयोगः Karma-yogaḥ stands for the sublime art of action without bondage — wherein duties are performed without attachment to outcome, and all fruits are surrendered to the Supreme.

It is the alchemy by which worldly engagement itself becomes a means to transcendence.

— ॐ —

निःश्रेयसकरौ (Niḥśreyasakarau):

Both paths are declared **निःश्रेयसकरौ** niḥśreyasakarau — productive of the highest welfare **निःश्रेयस** (niḥśreyasa)—that which leads beyond the transient good **प्रेयस्** (preyas) to the imperishable bliss of **मोक्ष** mokṣa.

The choice between the two is not of right and wrong but of our fitness and readiness.

— ॐ —

विशिष्यते (Viśiṣyate):

In pronouncing **विशिष्यते** viśiṣyate — that karma-yoga is the superior — Bhagwāna reveals that among seekers still in the domain of action and mind, active engagement without attachment is more accessible and thus more effective than the absolute renunciation which demands consummate inner purity.

We see how each word here unravels the luminous hierarchy of the two paths, speaking to the subtle gradations of spiritual ascent.

—: In Brief :—

— ॐ श्रीकृष्णाय नमः ॐ —

In this verse, Shri Krishna, the ever-compassionate guide of all seekers, addresses the question that weighed upon Arjuna's heart: the reconciliation of renunciation with action.

By declaring both **संन्यास** Sannyāsa and **कर्मयोग** Karma-Yoga as paths that culminate in liberation, the Lord affirms that each is rooted in detachment and the dissolution of ego—not in mere external form.

The term Sannyāsa here, as indicated by tradition and the context of the Gītā itself, must be understood not narrowly as the abandonment of outward activity, but as renunciation of the inner sense of doership, the ego's false claim over action.

Depending on context, the word "Sannyāsa" has been used in the Gītā in several nuanced ways—sometimes implying **ज्ञानयोग** Jnāna-yoga or the contemplative path **साङ्ख्ययोग** (Sāṅkhya-yoga), and elsewhere denoting mental relinquishment of attachment to the fruits of work.

Here, in harmony with verses that follow (5.4–5), Sannyāsa connotes the **साङ्ख्य-मार्ग** Sāṅkhya-mārga, the path of Knowledge which aims at renouncing all identification with the body and its workings, and resting in the Self as pure Consciousness.

— ॐ श्रीरामाय नमः ॐ —

Though both Sannyāsa and Karma-Yoga are independent paths to the same supreme end, Shri Krishna favors Karma-Yoga for the earnest seeker.

Why?

Because the path of inner renunciation while continuing outer action is safer and more accessible, especially for those not yet firmly established in Self-knowledge.

The path of pure Knowledge, though sublime, demands profound inner steadiness and a mind already withdrawn from sensory and mental activity. Absent such maturity, attempts at renunciation may lead to hypocrisy or inner turmoil.

The Karma-Yogī, by contrast, uses life itself as the field of sādhanā. He performs his duties without attachment, dedicating every act to the Divine as a यज्ञ Yajña, a sacred offering.

— ॐ परात्पराय नमः ॐ —

The Karma-Yogi neither craves success nor recoils from failure. By this steady practice, his heart is gradually purified, and in due time, true knowledge dawns of its own accord.

Indeed, in later verses, Shri Krishna declares that the Karma-Yogī reaches the same realization as the Jñānī, but with greater ease and stability.

The Karma-Yogī is not a mere doer, for he offers up every action to Bhagwāna Himself, surrendering both the fruits and the ego. Thus, he too is a Sannyāsī in the truest sense—renouncing internally, while serving outwardly.

Therefore, while both paths lead to mokṣa, it is Karma-Yoga, suffused with devotion, discernment, and detachment, that is most suited to the embodied being still active in the world.

Karma-Yoga is a beautiful path of synthesis, wherein action becomes a vehicle for transcendence. This is why Shri Krishna unequivocally declares it superior—not in theory, but in lived spiritual efficacy.

Salutations to the Karma-Yogi!

— ॐ त्रिगुणात्मकाय नमः ॐ —

Aye, let us sing our ode to the simple Sanātana-Dharmi — unwavering and steadfast in his dharma—who keeps humbly performing his ordained work in line with his वर्ण-आश्रम Varna-Āshram dharma day in and day out, looking neither for recognition nor reward—simply duty performed because that's what Krishna placed for him on his path.

— ॐ श्रीकृष्णाय नमः ॐ —

Salutations to the Soldiers of Sanātana-Dharma: Unsung Hero/Heroines!

Not robed in ochre, nor cloaked in hush—
but midst marketplace they tread,
Unseen, unpraised, disdained—yet staying unwavering and steadfast—
Heart afire with Dharma's flame.
No hermits of the hills—these are warrior set midst throngs of men,
Their deeds are Rites, each breath a Hymn,
their soul—a Shrine ever lit from within.

<u>Where others flinch at karma's snares,</u>
she strides through shadow bearing light;
No fruits she seeks, no rest she craves—her self she shed like shell in fight.
Unmoved by scorn, untouched by praise,
she serves, yet claims nor mark nor name;
Her life is dust, her heart Sanatan's flame—
the silent sanatani mother, unknown to fame.

<u>O who shall see 'em, veiled so plain?</u>
The world knows not their hidden greats—
Who fight for Dharma, remain in toil,
performing their duty decreed by fate—
Striding like the life-giving breeze—coursing through the mortal years.

<u>Lo, there they dwell:</u>
the true renunciants —of whom the world never knows,
Walking brisk in duty's light—
which 'sadhus' shirk, fearing dread karma's blots & shades.
Behold the true heroes: the sages none see, celebrate, or even know:
The simple householder men and women of Sanatana-Dharma, toiling daily
—performing their God-ordained duty, dharmas of Varna-Ashram.

— ॐ पारगाय नमः ॐ —

With this declaration in verse 5.2, the Lord-God Bhagwāna Shri Krishna has begun to weave the tapestry of unity between the contemplative and active paths, culminating in the vision that the true renunciant is not the one who abandons duty, but he who transcends attachment even while immersed in life's manifold works.

In the verses to come, Bhagwāna Shri Krishna will further reveal how this inner renunciation leads one to perceive the Self in all beings, and all beings in the Self — the sublime vision of the Sthitaprajña, the one established in the Eternal.

— ॐ तत सत ॐ —

Before we move on, let us bow in reverence to this sacred verse. Write it by hand, reflect on its meaning, chant it aloud, make it your own.

— ॐ —

श्रीभगवानुवाच -- śrībhagavānuvāca --

संन्यासः कर्मयोगश्च निःश्रेयसकरावुभौ ।
saṁnyāsaḥ karmayogaśca niḥśreyasakarāvubhau
तयोस्तु कर्मसंन्यासात्कर्मयोगो विशिष्यते ॥५-२॥
tayostu karmasaṁnyāsātkarmayogo viśiṣyate (5-2)

—ॐ—

श्रीभगवानुवाच -- śrībhagavānuvāca --

संन्यासः कर्मयोगश्च निःश्रेयसकरावुभौ ।

saṁnyāsaḥ karmayogaśca niḥśreyasakarāvubhau

तयोस्तु कर्मसंन्यासात्कर्मयोगो विशिष्यते ॥५-२॥

tayostu karmasaṁnyāsātkarmayogo viśiṣyate (5-2)

ॐ तत्सदिति श्रीमद्भगवद्गीतासूपनिषत्सु ब्रह्मविद्यायां योगशास्त्रे श्रीकृष्णार्जुनसंवादे
om tatsaditi śrīmadbhagavadgītāsūpaniṣatsu brahmavidyāyāṁ yogaśāstre śrīkṛṣṇārjunasaṁvāde
संन्यासयोगो नाम पञ्चमोऽध्यायः श्लोकः २
saṁnyāsayogo nāma pañcamo'dhyāyaḥ ślokaḥ 2

Om-Tat-Sat—Om (Braham) is the sole Reality. In the Yogic Scripture on the Science-of-Braham, the Shrimada-Bhāgvada-Gītā Upanishad, we hereby conclude Shloka 2 of the Dialogue between Shrī Krishna and Arjuna entitled Sanyāsa-Yoga, Canto V.

— ॐ श्रीपतये नमः ॐ —

Ode To The Karma-Yogi

As the lotus leaf repels the rain,
So too mud and sorrow glide away from the Karma-Yogi—
Staying unmarked by the tears of days and nights.

He does move through web of the wide, wild, world—
But stays uncaught, untouched.
He eats; he speaks; he toils in dust; he labors in some worldly field—
Yet no fruit from hand & deed, or harvest for himself, he seeks.

Each act, each breath of his—
Is an offering cast upon the altar of the Lord.
The world would press its thumbprint upon his soul—
But finds no purchase.

You do see him in sight, but he ain't quite there. Really, not quite—
A Witness aloof he abides in quiet stillness, performing his dharma.
Thusly lives a Karma-Yogi—always wrapped in bliss of Krishna.

But what of us?

Lovers of the fleeting,, we wed shadows.
Worship applause, build altars of ambition,
Chase praise—like a dog its tail—
Until weary, we one day lie in dust.
Aye... here lies the fool who spurned the Self—
And who lived a life unloved by his-self.

ॐ गीता श्लोकः ५.३ – GĪTĀ VERSE 5.3

ॐ श्रीमद्भगवद्गीतासूपनिषत्सु ब्रह्मविद्यायां योगशास्त्रे श्रीकृष्णार्जुनसंवादे
om śrīmadbhagavadgītāsūpaniṣatsu brahmavidyāyāṁ yogaśāstre śrīkṛṣṇārjunasaṁvāde
संन्यासयोगो नाम पञ्चमोऽध्यायः श्लोकः ३
saṁnyāsayogo nāma pañcamo'dhyāyaḥ ślokaḥ 3

— ॐ —

ज्ञेयः स नित्यसंन्यासी यो न द्वेष्टि न काङ्क्षति ।
jñeyaḥ sa nityasaṁnyāsī yo na dveṣṭi na kāṅkṣati
निर्द्वन्द्वो हि महाबाहो सुखं बन्धात्प्रमुच्यते ॥५-३॥
nirdvandvo hi mahābāho sukhaṁ bandhātpramucyate (5-3)

The Karma-Yogī, free of dualities, who neither hates nor desires, should be held to be a complete renunciant even though fully engaged in action, O mighty-armed; because one who is free of the pairs of opposites, stands freed of Karma's bondages as well. (5.3)

—: Word-by-Word :—

ज्ञेयः jñeyaḥ – to be known; सः saḥ – he; नित्यसंन्यासी nityasaṁnyāsī – as a perpetual renunciant; यः yaḥ – who; न dveṣṭi – does not hate; न kāṅkṣati – does not desire; निर्द्वन्द्वः nirdvandvaḥ – free from dualities; हि hi – indeed; महाबाहो mahābāho – O mighty-armed (Arjuna); सुखम् sukhaṁ – easily; बन्धात् bandhāt – from bondage; प्रमुच्यते pramucyate – is liberated.

—: Understanding The Verse :—

— ॐ त्रिलोकरक्षकाय नमः ॐ —

In this verse, Bhagwāna Shri Krishna offers a deeper insight into the true nature of सन्यास Sannyāsa, or renunciation.

Here, renunciation is not defined by the cessation of action, nor by external monastic formalities, but by the purity of the inner disposition — particularly the absence of राग द्वेश rāga and dveṣa, attachment and aversion.

O world, the one who moves through the world without being tossed by the dualities of pleasure and pain, gain and loss, honour and dishonour—he is, in truth, a renunciate — even if outwardly engaged in worldly actions!

Such a person, says Shri Krishna, is free from the bondage of karma not because he avoids work, but because he transcends its binding power by overcoming inner dualities.

This verse further affirms the theme of the Gītā: true liberation is an inner achievement, not a mere external arrangement. Thus, the verse continues to elevate Karma-Yoga by revealing its hidden renunciatory power.

—: Key Sanskrit Terms :—

Let us draw forth the soul of the verse by contemplating its Sanskrit lifeblood—those ancient words that flow quietly beneath the surface, bearing the fragrance of far-off heights.

— ॐ —

ज्ञेयः (Jñeyaḥ):

The term ज्ञेयः jñeyaḥ — "to be known" or "to be understood" — points towards a revelation of true vision.

Krishna here sets before the seeker a mark, a true standard of the realized sage, indicating not a theoretical understanding but the deep ज्ञान दृष्टिः jñāna-dṛṣṭi (sight of wisdom) that sees beyond mere appearances.

— ॐ —

नित्यसंन्यासी (Nityasaṁnyāsī):

A profound phrase, नित्यसंन्यासी nitya-saṁnyāsī indicates the one who is ever a renunciant — not merely by external abandonment, but through the eternal severance of inner attachment.

संन्यास Saṁnyāsa here is the perpetual renunciation of clinging and aversion, of desire and hatred, irrespective of outward activity.

— ॐ —

यो न द्वेष्टि न काङ्क्षति (Yo na dveṣṭi na kāṅkṣati):

The essence of नित्यसंन्यास nitya-saṁnyāsa lies here: "one who neither hates nor desires."

द्वेश Dveṣa (hatred) and काङ्क्ष kāṅkṣā (longing) are twin currents that bind the mind to संसार saṁsāra. To transcend both is to stand in equanimity समचित्तत्व (samacittatva), untouched by the play of opposites.

— ॐ —

निर्द्वन्द्वः (Nirdvandvaḥ):

The निर्द्वन्द्वः nirdvandvaḥ — the one free from dualities — has risen above pleasure and pain, gain and loss, praise and blame.

Dwelling beyond the flickering shadows of द्वन्द्व dvandva (dualities), such a soul abides in the tranquility of the Self.

— ॐ —

सुखं बन्धात् प्रमुच्यते (Sukhaṁ bandhāt pramucyate):

Sweet and natural — सुखं sukhaṁ — is the release from bondage for such a one.

No struggle, no conflict — liberation unfolds like the blossoming of a lotus untouched by the mud. For bondage itself was born only from clinging to the unreal; and when dualities are transcended, the chains fall away effortlessly.

Each term here has breathed to us an exalted vision of inner renunciation — a renunciation not of life, but of bondage to its illusions.

—: In Brief :—

— ॐ श्रीकृष्णाय नमः ॐ —

Bhagwāna Shri Krishna has unveiled the secret of true renunciation: it is not defined by outward withdrawal, but by inner equanimity. The one who performs his duties, yet remains untouched by the sway of opposites — who neither hates nor desires — is to be known as a true सन्यासी Sannyāsin, a renouncer in the deepest sense.

— ॐ श्रीरामाय नमः ॐ —

This verse must be seen in the light of what has been said previously: the external relinquishment of action does not automatically free one from bondage. What binds the soul is not the action itself, but the attachment to it, the identification with it as "mine" or "I am the doer."

The Karma-Yogī, though active in the world, performs all actions with inner detachment, offering them as sacred service to the Supreme. Thus, he is already free from karma's entangling net.

Shri Krishna refers to such a person as being "free from the pairs of opposites."

These द्वन्द्व dvandvas — such as joy and sorrow, gain and loss, praise and blame — are the ever-turning wheel of संसार saṃsāra.

As long as the soul is caught in preference and aversion, it remains bound to karma and the cycle of rebirth. But when the yogī neither pursues nor avoids, when he acts without ego and expectation, the polarities of the world no longer bind him.

Such a one has pierced the veils of माया māyā and stands established in the Self.

— ॐ चिरंजीविने नमः ॐ —

Indeed, attachment and aversion are the most insidious obstacles on the spiritual path. They color perception, distort judgment, and keep the heart fettered to transient objects.

As Shri Krishna teaches elsewhere, these are born of contact with the guṇas and must be endured and transcended through steadfastness धृति (dhṛti) and discrimination विवेक (viveka).

The Karma-Yogī, fortified by such inner strength, becomes like the lotus leaf — in the water, yet untouched by it.

In declaring such a Karma-Yogī to be the true Sannyāsin, Shri Krishna also challenges the misconception that only the one who physically renounces is spiritually advanced. Rather, Krishna glorifies interior renunciation as supreme — the state of being inwardly free, regardless of one's outer station in life.

— ॐ सत्यपराक्रमाय नमः ॐ —

Lord-God Bhagwāna Shri Krishna is not merely establishing the practical superiority of Karma-Yoga; He is revealing its spiritual profundity. Far from being a preliminary stage, it is a complete path in itself — one that leads to inner stillness, purification, and ultimately, liberation.

In the verses that follow, Shri Krishna will draw together the paths of Knowledge and Action, showing how both converge in the same vision of the Self — pointing to the unity that lies beyond all apparent distinctions.

— ॐ तत सत ॐ —

Before moving on, let us once more bow in deep reverence before this sacred verse of the Bhagavad-Gītā, an eternal beacon of wisdom that ceaselessly illumines the path of seekers. Engage with its form—inscribe it with your own hand, let your heart dwell upon its meaning, and raise your voice in its chanting—for within these syllables echoes the undying proclamation delivered millennia ago on the battlefield of Kurukshetra. These words, transmitted unchanged across the unbroken chain of generations, form a living bridge, linking us to that sanctified era when Bhagwāna Shri Krishna Himself walked this earth and bestowed this divine teaching. Through the luminous vibration of these sacred Sanskrit sounds, we are drawn nearer to His timeless presence, touching the very heartbeat of the Eternal.

— ॐ —

ज्ञेयः स नित्यसंन्यासी यो न द्वेष्टि न काङ्क्षति ।
jñeyaḥ sa nityasaṁnyāsī yo na dveṣṭi na kāṅkṣati
निर्द्वन्द्वो हि महाबाहो सुखं बन्धात्प्रमुच्यते ॥५-३॥
nirdvandvo hi mahābāho sukhaṁ bandhātpramucyate (5-3)

— ॐ —

ज्ञेयः स नित्यसंन्यासी यो न द्वेष्टि न काङ्क्षति ।
jñeyaḥ sa nityasaṁnyāsī yo na dveṣṭi na kāṅkṣati
निर्द्वन्द्वो हि महाबाहो सुखं बन्धात्प्रमुच्यते ॥५-३॥
nirdvandvo hi mahābāho sukhaṁ bandhātpramucyate (5-3)

ॐ तत्सदिति श्रीमद्भगवद्गीतासूपनिषत्सु ब्रह्मविद्यायां योगशास्त्रे श्रीकृष्णार्जुनसंवादे
om tatsaditi śrīmadbhagavadgītāsūpaniṣatsu brahmavidyāyāṁ yogaśāstre śrīkṛṣṇārjunasaṁvāde
संन्यासयोगो नाम पञ्चमोऽध्यायः श्लोकः ३
saṁnyāsayogo nāma pañcamo'dhyāyaḥ ślokaḥ 3

Om-Tat-Sat—Om (Braham) is the sole Reality. In the Yogic Scripture on the Science-of-Braham, the Shrimada-Bhāgvada-Gītā Upanishad, we hereby conclude Shloka 3 of the Dialogue between Shrī Krishna and Arjuna entitled Sanyāsa-Yoga, Canto V.

— ॐ सर्वपालकाय नमः ॐ —

O fool, stop this Day-dreaming of Reaching God, doing Nothing.
Thou canst soar to heaven by wishing wings to grow.
Nor leap unto great heights by gathering wool in dream.
There's a Ladder to the Highest-Realm: the ladder of Dharmika-Karma.
Aye, the rooftop of true renunciation remains far above—
it ain't below -- for display & mockery that's seen midst Charlatans & Frauds.

With hands in service steeped, one must ascend the ladder rung by rung,
Ere standing still in Krishna's Realm,
where none are praised and none are sung.

Renunciation is reached by first performing Karma.
And Dharmika duties & deeds, are like the steps well laid,
Which alone shape the soul for higher-realms.

Remember: Varna-Ashram's sacred ways, well-trod,
Are steps that lead thee straight near to God.
And whosoever diligently climbs with true steadfast heart,
Will find the sky no longer blue—
For he will have reached the resplendent zone,
The supernal realm beyond names & forms.

O mortal: Karma-Yoga is that stairway
which places thee at the Portal-to-Eternal.

Renounce fully?
Aye, but only in the last quarter of life.
For to leap too soon is fraught with fall,
And to first serve Sanātana-Dharma is to rise aright.

The hypocrite says: "I renounce,"
then keeps running around for sustenance, shelter, alms throughout life,
Though staying clinging to the world in a thousand ways—
the fools calls his life an offering to God!

ॐ गीता श्लोकः ५.४ – GĪTĀ VERSE 5.4

ॐ श्रीमद्भगवद्गीतासूपनिषत्सु ब्रह्मविद्यायां योगशास्त्रे श्रीकृष्णार्जुनसंवादे
om śrīmadbhagavadgītāsūpaniṣatsu brahmavidyāyāṁ yogaśāstre śrīkṛṣṇārjunasaṁvāde
संन्यासयोगो नाम पञ्चमोऽध्यायः श्लोकः ४
saṁnyāsayogo nāma pañcamo'dhyāyaḥ ślokaḥ 4

— ॐ —

साङ्ख्ययोगौ पृथग्बालाः प्रवदन्ति न पण्डिताः ।
sāṅkhyayogau pṛthagbālāḥ pravadanti na paṇḍitāḥ
एकमप्यास्थितः सम्यगुभयोर्विन्दते फलम् ॥५-४॥
ekamapyāsthitaḥ samyagubhayorvindate phalam (5-4)

It is the ignorant who perceives Sānkhya-Yoga and Karma-Yoga as leading to different outcomes—but not so the wise. Firmly established in even one, one obtains the fruit of both. (5.4)

—: Word-by-Word :—

साङ्ख्ययोगौ sāṅkhyayogau – the paths of sankhya (knowledge) and karma-yoga; पृथक् pṛthak – as distinct; बालाः bālāḥ – the unenlightened; प्रवदन्ति pravadanti – speak of; न na – not; पण्डिताः paṇḍitāḥ – the wise; एकम् ekam – even one; अपि api – indeed; आस्थितः āsthitaḥ – established in; सम्यक् samyak – properly; उभयोः ubhayoḥ – of both; विन्दते vindate – attains; फलम् phalam – the result.

—: Understanding The Verse :—

— ॐ श्रीकृष्णाय नमः ॐ —

In this verse, Bhagwāna Shri Krishna addresses a subtle but significant misconception that arises in the spiritual mind: the perceived division between the path of साङ्ख्योग Sānkhya (the Yoga of Knowledge) and the path of कर्मयोग Karma-Yoga (the Yoga of Action).

Superficially, these may appear as divergent approaches — one marked by contemplative renunciation and the other by dynamic engagement.

Yet the Lord makes it unequivocally clear: only those of immature understanding perceive them as leading to different ends. The wise, by contrast, discern their essential unity.

Both paths, when followed with steadfastness and right understanding, lead the seeker to the same supreme goal — Self-realization and liberation मोक्ष (mokṣa). Thus, Krishna affirms the intrinsic non-duality of spiritual means, even when their external modes of expression differ.

—: Key Sanskrit Terms :—

Focusing on its pivotal Sanskrit terms, let us quietly illuminate the depth of this verse—which is as if twin rivers merging. Every word here flows in concert—dissolving differences into unity – even as the wise also see sannyāsa and karma-yoga not as separate, but one.

— ॐ —

साङ्ख्ययोगौ (Sāṅkhyayogau)—meaning साङ्ख्य Sāṅkhya and योग yoga.

Important: Here, साङ्ख्य Sāṅkhya refers to the path of knowledge ज्ञान-मार्ग (jñāna-mārga)—where discrimination (viveka) and renunciation lead the seeker to realize the Self as distinct from प्रकृति prakṛti.

And योग Yoga refers to कर्मयोग Karmayoga, the offering of actions without attachment. Though their methods seem distinct — contemplation versus action — both ascend toward the same summit: liberation.

— ॐ —

पृथक् (Pṛthak):

पृथक् Pṛthak means "as separate," "as different."

The spiritually immature perceive these two paths as fundamentally divided, unable to see the hidden unity that underlies the diversity of approaches in Dharma.

— ॐ —

बालाः (Bālāḥ):

The बालाः "bālāḥ" — literally "children" — are not defined by age but by the immaturity of soul-understanding.

The immature see the surface distinctions of the paths, but not their inner harmony.

Spiritual childhood is marked by division; spiritual wisdom by synthesis.

— ॐ —

पण्डिताः (Paṇḍitāḥ):

The पण्डिताः paṇḍitāḥ, the wise, are not merely scholars but seers whose knowledge is ripened by realization.

To them, differences of method are but variations of one central truth: the uncovering of the Self.

— ॐ —

सम्यक् (Samyak) and आस्थितः (Āsthitaḥ):

One who is सम्यक्-आस्थितः samyak-āsthitaḥ — "rightly established" — even in one path, faithfully and with right understanding, attains the fruits of both.

For truth is one; only the approaches vary according to the temperament and stage of the seeker.

Every word of this verse delicately reveals the deeper unity hidden beneath the apparent diversity of spiritual paths in Sanātana-Dharma.

—: *In Brief* :—

— ॐ श्रीकृष्णाय नमः ॐ —

Bhagwāna Shri Krishna here dispels the false dichotomy that often clouds the spiritual aspirant's understanding. He declares: "It is the ignorant, not the wise, who believe that साङ्ख्य Sānkhya and कर्मयोग Karma-Yoga yield different results." This confusion arises from judging by outward forms and failing to perceive the inner unity of purpose that animates both paths.

Indeed, the path of साङ्ख्य Sānkhya, which is centered on the cultivation of discriminative knowledge विवेक (viveka) and Self-abidance, and the path of Karma-Yoga, which is rooted in action performed without attachment, are two expressions of the same inward striving toward God-realization.

Both disciplines, though differing in method, ultimately culminate in the direct perception of the Self आत्म-ज्ञान (ātma-jñāna) and the dissolution of egoic bondage.

— ॐ श्रीरामाय नमः ॐ —

The unwise — those who yet stay entangled in conceptual distinctions — imagine that ज्ञान Jñāna and कर्म Karma are mutually exclusive or opposed. But this is not so.

The पण्डिताः Panditaḥ, the truly wise, see no such separation. For them, the river of Karma and the river of Jñāna both merge in the ocean of the Supreme.

— ॐ परस्मै ज्योतिषे नमः ॐ —

This verse proclaims a powerful truth: "One who is firmly established in either path attains the fruit of both." This is not a vague metaphysical statement, but a declaration of spiritual law.

The Karma-Yogī, through the purification of the heart and surrender of the fruits of action, becomes fit for Knowledge, and in time, attains it naturally.

Conversely, the Jñāna-Yogī, by dwelling steadily in the Self, naturally renounces all action born of ego — thus, he fulfills Karma-Yoga inwardly, even while outwardly inactive.

— ॐ अनन्ताय नमः ॐ —

Indeed, it is through this convergence that the Gītā reveals its profound harmonization of the two great currents in spiritual life: knowledge and action.

Though the साधना sādhana (discipline) of each path may seem distinct, their fruit is one and the same — the realization of the Eternal, the vision of the Self in all beings and all beings in the Self.

Moreover, if साङ्ख्ययोग Sānkhya-Yoga and कर्मयोग Karma-Yoga were not independently efficacious — if one were merely a precursor to the other — then the Lord's assertion that either alone suffices would lose its significance. But Bhagwāna Shri Krishna affirms that each path is complete in itself and leads, when practiced to perfection, to the highest goal.

— ॐ श्रीकृष्णगोपालाय नमः ॐ —

Remember: There's a fire that consumes fuel—which leads to that fire which needs no fuel.
The कर्म योगी Karma-Yogī burns karma through the fuel of action;
the साङ्ख्य योगी Sānkhya-Yogī burns it through the fuel of wisdom.
In the end, both lead to the realm where is found burning only the pure flame: the fiery flame of pure consciousness.

— ॐ दयासाराय नमः ॐ —

What is Arjuna's Dilemma and the Gitā's Solution?
Arjuna is torn between contemplation and action—that is the ever present dilemma in everyone's life;
and what is being taught by Bhagwāna Shri Krishna is that even the gory bloody field of battle—when entered having first surrendered to Krishna—becomes an arena of divine realization.
That then is the solution.
Indeed, when the Jnāna of Gitā is taken to be the solution, then all the dilemmas of life disappear.

— ॐ दयासाराय नमः ॐ —

This verse bridges the perceived gap between renunciation and action, contemplation and engagement.

The Gītā's teaching is not one of exclusion but of integration — a synthesis that uplifts both the contemplative sage and the devoted servant into the unity of the Divine.

In the next verse, Shri Krishna will continue to elaborate this harmony, showing how the perfected seeker on either path arrives at the same non-dual realization, wherein all distinctions vanish, and only the Self remains.

— ॐ तत सत ॐ —

Before we move on, let us bow in reverence to this sacred verse—a timeless beacon of wisdom guiding seekers for ages. Write it by hand, reflect on its meaning, and chant it aloud, for these sounds alone carry the authenticity of that era. The world may have changed but the living vibration of these Sanskrit sounds still remain as original as they were when Bhagwān Shri Krishna Himself walked the earth and imparted these teachings.

— ॐ —

साङ्ख्ययोगौ पृथग्बालाः प्रवदन्ति न पण्डिताः ।
sāṅkhyayogau pṛthagbālāḥ pravadanti na paṇḍitāḥ
एकमप्यास्थितः सम्यगुभयोर्विन्दते फलम् ॥५-४॥
ekamapyāsthitaḥ samyagubhayorvindate phalam (5-4)

— ॐ —

साङ्ख्ययोगौ पृथग्बालाः प्रवदन्ति न पण्डिताः ।
sāṅkhyayogau pṛthagbālāḥ pravadanti na paṇḍitāḥ
एकमप्यास्थितः सम्यगुभयोर्विन्दते फलम् ॥५-४॥
ekamapyāsthitaḥ samyagubhayorvindate phalam (5-4)

ॐ तत्सदिति श्रीमद्भगवद्गीतासूपनिषत्सु ब्रह्मविद्यायां योगशास्त्रे श्रीकृष्णार्जुनसंवादे
om tatsaditi śrīmadbhagavadgītāsūpaniṣatsu brahmavidyāyāṁ yogaśāstre śrīkṛṣṇārjunasaṁvāde
संन्यासयोगो नाम पञ्चमोऽध्यायः श्लोकः ४
saṁnyāsayogo nāma pañcamo'dhyāyaḥ ślokaḥ 4

Om-Tat-Sat—Om (Braham) is the sole Reality. In the Yogic Scripture on the Science-of-Braham, the Shrimada-Bhāgvada-Gītā Upanishad, we hereby conclude Shloka 4 of the Dialogue between Shrī Krishna and Arjuna entitled Sanyāsa-Yoga, Canto V.

— ॐ श्रीसीतारक्षाय नमः ॐ —

He who, with quiet strength, subdues the storm of ire and desire,
Whose heart stays unshaken and quiet—
— even midst dance of world's infinite desires —
He walks no more the path of death—
He climbs to a realm infinitely higher.

— o —

Not grasp, nor gold, nor fleeting thrill ever makes him stray;
True peace, untouched by gain & loss, is his—
who learns to says "No" — manages to turn away.
Only in silence blooms that deathless Bliss—
which no night can ever betray.

ॐ गीता श्लोकः ५.५ – GĪTĀ VERSE 5.5

ॐ श्रीमद्भगवद्गीतासूपनिषत्सु ब्रह्मविद्यायां योगशास्त्रे श्रीकृष्णार्जुनसंवादे
om śrīmadbhagavadgītāsūpaniṣatsu brahmavidyāyāṁ yogaśāstre śrīkṛṣṇārjunasaṁvāde
संन्यासयोगो नाम पञ्चमोऽध्यायः श्लोकः ५
saṁnyāsayogo nāma pañcamo'dhyāyaḥ ślokaḥ 5

— ॐ —

यत्साङ्ख्यैः प्राप्यते स्थानं तद्योगैरपि गम्यते ।
yatsāṅkhyaiḥ prāpyate sthānaṁ tadyogairapi gamyate
एकं साङ्ख्यं च योगं च यः पश्यति स पश्यति ॥५-५॥
ekaṁ sāṅkhyaṁ ca yogaṁ ca yaḥ paśyati sa paśyati (5-5)

That sovereign state which is reached by the Sānkhya-Yogī, is attained by the Karma-Yogī as well. He who sees the Path of Sankhya (Knowledge) and the Path of Karma (performing ones ordained duty in line with Varna-Āshram Dharma) to be one and the same, he truly sees. (5.5)

—: Word-by-Word :—

यत् yat – which; साङ्ख्यैः sāṅkhyaiḥ – by the path of knowledge; प्राप्यते prāpyate – is attained; स्थानम् sthānam – the state; तत् tat – that; योगैः yogaiḥ – by the path of karma-yoga; अपि api – also; गम्यते gamyate – is reached; एकम् ekam – one; साङ्ख्यम् sāṅkhyam – knowledge; च ca – and; योगम् yogam – performing ordained karma ; यः yaḥ – who; पश्यति paśyati – sees; सः saḥ – he; पश्यति paśyati – truly sees.

—: Understanding The Verse :—

— ॐ श्रीकृष्णाय नमः ॐ —

In this verse, Bhagwāna Shri Krishna continues His discourse on the essential unity of the spiritual paths, affirming that the supreme goal reached by the साङ्ख्य योगी Sānkhya-Yogī—the contemplative knower of the Self—is equally attained by the कर्मयोगी Karma-Yogī, the performer of action for duty's sake.

While the two paths differ in their mode of practice—one being inward and reflective, the other outward and dynamic—their ultimate fruition is the same: liberation मोक्ष (mokṣa), the realization of the eternal Self.

Shri Krishna further declares: he alone truly sees, who perceives both paths as leading to the same transcendent state.

Thus this verse offers a profound spiritual synthesis, dissolving the apparent opposition between renunciation and engagement, contemplation and action. It extols the spiritual unity underlying the diversity of disciplines seen in Sanātana-Dharma.

— ॐ श्रीरामाय नमः ॐ —

The Clay and Its Forms

Whether molded into a pot (कर्म karma) or left unshaped (ज्ञान jnana), the essence remains clay—so too, whether engaged in action or immersed in wisdom, the realized being abides in the One Truth.

And thee O mortal should never stay forgetful of this truth: We are but clay in the hand of fate—it is Krishna's will which ultimately decides what each of us does become.

Alas, some of us are destined to be forged in the intense fire of gruelling karmas—and ours is but to do and die, and whining and bemoaning our fate is of no avail; grin and bear it.

— ॐ श्रीकृष्णाय नमः ॐ —

I am an Instrument in His Hand

Formed by His hand, I rise, I fall—
—placed in fire, or bathed in rain.
The pot complains not of the wheel—
nor of the kiln, nor of the strain.

In each twist and tempering of my fate,
the Maker's plan alone I see,
And thus I yield to every stroke—
for He Krishna alone knows what shall be.

I am but a vessel shaped by His will—
His fingers alone guide all my curls and kinks.
My hollowness is not just simply a flaw—
it's a space He placed—to hold, perhaps,
a few nectar-beads.

The Karma-Yogi surrenders—
not to 'fate', but to Krishna's design;
He acts not for himself,
rather he functions—as an earthen serving-cup of His:
To be simply broken -- or be supped by the Divine,
at His pleasure and Will
—After all... this is all just a Leela of His.

Hearken, O mortal:

To yield to God is not to lose our form—
But have our life touched by the shaping grace of Krishn.

—: Key Sanskrit Terms :—

Now let's us approach the verse with care, allowing its principal Sanskrit expressions to guide us toward the inner core.

— ॐ —

यत् साङ्ख्यैः प्राप्यते स्थानम् (Yat sāṅkhyaiḥ prāpyate sthānam):

The स्थानम् sthānaṁ — the sovereign state, the firm station of the Self — is the culmination of the साङ्ख्य sāṅkhya path: pure Self-realization, free from duality and becoming.

Here, प्राप्यते prāpyate suggests not the gaining of something new, but the unveiling of what is ever-present — the immortal essence of being.

— ॐ —

तत् योगैः अपि गम्यते (Tat yogaiḥ api gamyate):

What the path of knowledge attains, the path of karma-yoga also reaches गम्यते (gamyate). Gamyate ("is attained") subtly suggests a journey — not spatial, but of inward ripening, where the doer is purified into the knower.

— ॐ —

एकं साङ्ख्यं च योगं च (Ekaṁ sāṅkhyaṁ ca yogaṁ ca):

The vision of oneness एकं (ekaṁ) between साङ्ख्य Sāṅkhya and योग Yoga is the heart of this śloka.

They are not two, but different doors opening into the same sanctuary of the spirit.

Both paths dissolve the illusion of separateness and lead to the one indivisible Reality.

— ॐ —

यः पश्यति सः पश्यति (Yaḥ paśyati saḥ paśyati):

A phrase of deep resonance: "He who sees, truly sees."

पश्यति Paśyati here is not ordinary seeing, but ज्ञान-दृष्टि jñāna-dṛṣṭi — the eye of wisdom.

It is not an intellectual conclusion, but the seer's direct, luminous realization of truth beyond the veils of appearance.

Each phrase in this verse carefully interlaces the profound truth: that the paths of Sanātana-Dharma are many, but the goal is one, and true vision lies in perceiving their essential unity.

—: In Brief :—

— ॐ श्रीकृष्णाय नमः ॐ —

Bhagwāna Shri Krishna here confirms the central truth which was introduced in the previous verse and now brought to radiant clarity: the supreme state परम स्थानं (param sthānam)—the state of unbroken union with the Self—is equally accessible through Sānkhya-Yoga, the path of Knowledge, and through Karma-Yoga, the path of performing one's ordained dharma.

— ॐ श्रीरामाय नमः ॐ —

Though their disciplines may appear to diverge in method—the one emphasizing discrimination विवेक (viveka) and the stilling of the mind, the other dedication of action and renunciation of fruits—their destination is one and the same.

It is the transcendence of ego, the dissolution of ignorance, and the direct realization of the Ātmā, the inner Self untouched by change or sorrow.

Shri Krishna states, "He truly sees, who sees Sānkhya and Yoga as one"—thus honoring the vision of the wise पण्डिताः (paṇḍitaḥ), who see beyond the surface forms into the essence of साधना sādhanā.

To see rightly is to perceive unity in diversity, to recognize that all true paths, when pursued with purity and sincerity, lead to the One Reality.

— ॐ गीताचार्याय नमः ॐ —

Just as rivers, though flowing from different directions, ultimately merge into the ocean, so do these two noble paths—साङ्ख्य Sānkhya and कर्मयोग Karma-Yoga—converge in the boundless ocean of Self-realization.

Their practices may be distinct, yet their culmination is in non-duality: the annihilation of ignorance, the awakening into Braham.

The analogy offered by the wise is so compelling: just as a traveler can reach the same city either by journeying eastward or westward, so too can the spiritual aspirant attain the supreme Reality by either path—provided he adheres to it with unwavering determination and right understanding.

— ॐ कामविजयाय नमः ॐ —

This verse is also an exhortation to transcend sectarian or dogmatic thinking.

The Lord reveals here a universal truth that all paths grounded in Sanātana-Dharma and spiritual sincerity will lead to liberation when pursued to their end. What matters is clarity of vision, firmness of resolve, and purity of heart—and of course the fact that they must be grounded in Sanātana-Dharma, for there are so many acerbic vicious sects masquerading as religions—but of which religion, there is only one: the One and Only: एकं सनातन-धर्म Ekam-Sanātana-Dharma.

— ॐ सर्वपालकाय नमः ॐ —

While the Gītā elsewhere extols the practical accessibility of Karma-Yoga, here Shri Krishna places both disciplines on equal footing with regard to their goal. He affirms a vision of harmony rather than hierarchy, of inner unity rather than outward division.

This verse stands as a bright beacon of spiritual inclusiveness—declaring that all true Yoga, whether contemplative or active, ultimately leads to the same eternal Truth, when pursued with devotion, detachment, and discernment.

In the next verse, Shri Krishna will further elaborate on the inner transformation that arises when one is truly established in the Self, regardless of the external path pursued—a transformation that results in equanimity, peace, and the end of all bondage.

— ॐ तत सत ॐ —

Before moving on, let us once more bow in deep reverence before this sacred verse of the Bhagavad-Gītā, an eternal beacon of wisdom that ceaselessly illumines the path of seekers. Engage with its form—inscribe it with your own hand, let your heart dwell upon its meaning, and raise your voice in its chanting—for within these syllables echoes the undying proclamation delivered millennia ago on the battlefield of Kurukshetra. These words, transmitted unchanged across the unbroken chain of generations, form a living bridge, linking us to that sanctified era when Bhagwāna Shri Krishna Himself walked this earth and bestowed this divine teaching. Through the luminous vibration of these sacred Sanskrit sounds, we are drawn nearer to His timeless presence, touching the very heartbeat of the Eternal.

— ॐ —

यत्साङ्ख्यैः प्राप्यते स्थानं तद्योगैरपि गम्यते ।
yatsāṅkhyaiḥ prāpyate sthānaṁ tadyogairapi gamyate
एकं साङ्ख्यं च योगं च यः पश्यति स पश्यति ॥५-५॥
ekaṁ sāṅkhyaṁ ca yogaṁ ca yaḥ paśyati sa paśyati (5-5)

—ॐ—

यत्साङ्ख्यैः प्राप्यते स्थानं तद्योगैरपि गम्यते ।
yatsāṅkhyaiḥ prāpyate sthānaṁ tadyogairapi gamyate
एकं साङ्ख्यं च योगं च यः पश्यति स पश्यति ॥५-५॥
ekaṁ sāṅkhyaṁ ca yogaṁ ca yaḥ paśyati sa paśyati (5-5)

ॐ तत्सदिति श्रीमद्भगवद्गीतासूपनिषत्सु ब्रह्मविद्यायां योगशास्त्रे श्रीकृष्णार्जुनसंवादे
om tatsaditi śrīmadbhagavadgītāsūpaniṣatsu brahmavidyāyāṁ yogaśāstre śrīkṛṣṇārjunasaṁvāde
संन्यासयोगो नाम पञ्चमोऽध्यायः श्लोकः ५
saṁnyāsayogo nāma pañcamo'dhyāyaḥ ślokaḥ 5

Om-Tat-Sat—Om (Braham) is the sole Reality. In the Yogic Scripture on the Science-of-Braham, the Shrimada-Bhāgvada-Gītā Upanishad, we hereby conclude Shloka 5 of the Dialogue between Shrī Krishna and Arjuna entitled Sanyāsa-Yoga, Canto V.

— ॐ यतिरूपाय नमः ॐ —

The Twin-Named Single Path

Yes sirree bob! This is a threshold verse—
Where the mask begins to fall;
Where man sheds not blood, but hisself—his mind!
And with the mind died—
—By the path-of-Sankhya or path-of-Karma, take thy pick, O seeker—
he re-becomes his True-Self again: the ātmā .
Yes sir, the Karma-Yogi fought most ferociously;
But no sir, he was not slain in the battle,
Rather he become silenced—by an untold bliss supreme—
Just as was the Sankhya-Yogi before him.

At the Core, They Are Really Not Two.

The Sānkhya-Yogī sees—and lets go.
The Karma-Yogī gives—and forgets.
Different hands, bearing the same flame.
Only the deluded asks:
"Which path, O sir, is better, higher?"

ॐ गीता श्लोकः ५.६ – GĪTĀ VERSE 5.6

ॐ श्रीमद्भगवद्गीतासूपनिषत्सु ब्रह्मविद्यायां योगशास्त्रे श्रीकृष्णार्जुनसंवादे
om śrīmadbhagavadgītāsūpaniṣatsu brahmavidyāyāṁ yogaśāstre śrīkṛṣṇārjunasaṁvāde
संन्यासयोगो नाम पञ्चमोऽध्यायः श्लोकः ६
saṁnyāsayogo nāma pañcamo'dhyāyaḥ ślokaḥ 6

— ॐ —

संन्यासस्तु महाबाहो दुःखमाप्तुमयोगतः ।
saṁnyāsastu mahābāho duḥkhamāptumayogataḥ
योगयुक्तो मुनिर्ब्रह्म नचिरेणाधिगच्छति ॥५-६॥
yogayukto munirbrahma nacireṇādhigacchati (5-6)

But renunciation of action is difficult to attain without performance of one's ordained dharma , O mighty-armed; whereas the sage who is devoted to performing one's ordained karma, is able to attain to Braham more speedily.
(5.6)

—: Word-by-Word :—

संन्यासः saṁnyāsaḥ – renunciation; तु tu – indeed; महाबाहो mahābāho – O mighty-armed (Arjuna); दुःखम् duḥkham – difficult; आप्तुम् āptum – to attain; अयोगतः ayogataḥ – without yoga; योगयुक्तः yogayuktaḥ – one engaged in yoga; मुनिः muniḥ – the sage; ब्रह्म brahma – Brahman; नचिरेण nacireṇa – without delay; अधिगच्छति adhigacchati – attains.

—: Understanding The Verse :—

— ॐ श्रीकृष्णाय नमः ॐ —

In this verse, Bhagwāna Shri Krishna continues to unfold the relationship between the path of renunciation सन्यास (Sannyāsa) and the path of performing one's ordained-dharma कर्मयोग (Karma-Yoga).

In fact Shri Krishna here makes an emphatic declaration: renunciation is difficult to attain without having first passed through the path of Karma-Yoga. He who is steadfast in Karma-Yoga, performing all duties in a spirit of offering, attains to Braham—the supreme, formless Reality—more swiftly and with far greater ease.

— ॐ श्रीरामाय नमः ॐ —

This verse subtly corrects the tendency of some aspirants to shun action prematurely, imagining that mere external renunciation is a faster or loftier route to Him.

Shri Krishna disabuses such notions by declaring that the inner purification and stability required for true renunciation are best cultivated through detached engagement with the world—following the path of one's वर्ण-आश्रम-धर्म Varna-Āshram Dharma.

It is only when the ego is cleansed through duty performed without desire that the seeker becomes fit for ज्ञानयोग Jnānayoga, the path of pure contemplation.

—: Key Sanskrit Terms :—

Now let us lean into the stillness that each Sanskrit word holds, and allow it to become a mirror—not of ideas alone, but of the one who gazes.

— ॐ —

संन्यासः (Saṁnyāsaḥ):

संन्यास Saṁnyāsa here refers not to a mere external abandonment of works but to the profound inner cessation of all desire-driven action — the dropping away of the ego's involvement in the play of प्रकृति prakṛti.

It is the culmination of inner renunciation, a life bathed in pure awareness.

— ॐ —

महाबाहो (Mahābāho):

Addressing Arjuna as महाबाहो mahābāho — mighty-armed — Shri Krishna invokes not only physical prowess but hints at the inner strength required to tread the subtle and arduous path of renunciation.

True renunciation demands a might greater than that of any battlefield — the conquest of the restless mind.

— ॐ —

दुःखम् आप्तुम् (Duḥkham āptum):

Without the preparatory purification that karma-yoga affords, the attempt at direct renunciation leads to दुःख duḥkha — sorrow, restlessness, inner conflict.

Renunciation without the maturity born of detached action is barren and painful, for the ego subtly lingers even in the garb of withdrawal.

— ॐ —

योगयुक्तः (Yogayuktaḥ):

The योगयुक्तः yogayuktaḥ — one who is firmly yoked to karma-yoga — performs actions without attachment, dedicating all works unto the Supreme.

Through such steady practice, the heart is cleansed, and the soul becomes fit for the higher ascent into Braham-awareness.

— ॐ —

मुनिः ब्रह्म अधिगच्छति (Munir brahma adhigacchati):

The मुनि muni — the silent sage, one who reflects and abides in the inner Self — attains अधिगच्छति (adhigacchati) Braham, the boundless, the changeless.

And नचिरेण nacireṇa — "without delay" — he arrives at that supreme station, for his being is ripened by the fire of purified action and inward stillness.

Behold how each phrase in this verse delicately illumines the necessary stages of the soul's journey: preparation through action, maturation into silence—and finally realization of the Eternal.

—: *In Brief* :—

— ॐ श्रीकृष्णाय नमः ॐ —

Here, Bhagwāna Shri Krishna draws attention to a deep spiritual truth often misunderstood by seekers: that true renunciation संन्यास (Sannyāsa) is not a matter of simply relinquishing outer activity, but of purifying the heart and mind, of dissolving attachments, aversions, and the sense of doership.

In fact such inner renunciation is exceedingly difficult to attain without first walking the path of Karma-Yoga.

— ॐ श्रीरामाय नमः ॐ —

Though Sannyāsa and Karma-Yoga both aim at the realization of Braham, the formless Absolute, the latter provides a practical foundation for the former.

Karma-Yoga prepares the inner being—by steadying the senses, restraining the mind, and relinquishing the craving for fruits of action. The performance of duty as a sacred यज्ञ Yajña purifies the intellect, and gradually leads one to the stillness wherein Braham is known.

— ॐ दण्डकारण्यवासीने नमः ॐ —

The phrase योगयुक्तः मुनिः "Yoga-yuktaḥ muniḥ" refers to the wise and disciplined Karma-Yogī, one who performs all actions with detachment, equanimity, and a consciousness of the Divine.

Such a person is not disturbed by success or failure, not swayed by gain or loss, for his actions are performed in dedication to the Lord, and not for personal gratification. This steadfastness in Yoga—rooted in dharma and devotion—leads him swiftly to the realization of Braham.

It is worth noting that in this context, the word ब्रह्म 'Braham' refers not merely to a metaphysical abstraction, but to the living, infinite Reality that is the source, support, and substratum of all existence.

To "attain Braham" ब्रह्म अधिगच्छति means to awaken to the truth of one's own Self as non-different from Braham, beyond all dualities and limitations.

— ॐ रामानुजप्रियाय नमः ॐ —

By addressing Arjuna as महाबाहो Mahābāhu—"mighty-armed"—Shri Krishna not only praises his physical strength but subtly reminds him of his inner strength and spiritual potential.

It is as though the Lord is saying, "O strong-armed warrior, do not fear the path of Karma-Yoga; it is the surest and swiftest means to the highest realization for one like you, still engaged in the world."

— ॐ परिपूर्णतमाय नमः ॐ —

This verse also continues to affirm a key teaching of the Gītā: that renunciation through right action is superior to renunciation through abstention.

The Karma-Yogī does not abandon the world; rather, he transforms his relationship with it. He sees the Divine in all beings, performs every action as an offering to that Divine, and thereby dissolves the ego, which is the true obstacle to liberation.

Shri Krishna urges not withdrawal, but transformation. One need not retire to the forest or shun all duties; one must rather change the interior motive—from ego to offering, from self-centered desire to God-centered devotion. This inner shift leads the seeker swiftly to ब्रह्म साक्षात्कार Brahma-sākṣātkāra, the direct realization of the Infinite.

In later verses, Bhagwāna will unveil how one who has attained Braham sees the Self in all beings, and abides in perfect peace.

— ॐ तत सत ॐ —

Before we move on, let us bow in reverence to this sacred verse. Write it by hand, reflect on its meaning, chant it aloud, make it your own.

— ॐ —

संन्यासस्तु महाबाहो दुःखमाप्तुमयोगतः ।
samnyāsastu mahābāho duḥkhamāptumayogataḥ
योगयुक्तो मुनिर्ब्रह्म नचिरेणाधिगच्छति ॥५-६॥
yogayukto munirbrahma nacireṇādhigacchati (5-6)

संन्यासस्तु महाबाहो दुःखमाप्तुमयोगतः ।
saṁnyāsastu mahābāho duḥkhamāptumayogataḥ
योगयुक्तो मुनिर्ब्रह्म नचिरेणाधिगच्छति ॥५-६॥
yogayukto munirbrahma nacireṇādhigacchati (5-6)

ॐ तत्सदिति श्रीमद्भगवद्गीतासूपनिषत्सु ब्रह्मविद्यायां योगशास्त्रे श्रीकृष्णार्जुनसंवादे
om tatsaditi śrīmadbhagavadgītāsūpaniṣatsu brahmavidyāyāṁ yogaśāstre śrīkṛṣṇārjunasaṁvāde
संन्यासयोगो नाम पञ्चमोऽध्यायः श्लोकः ६
saṁnyāsayogo nāma pañcamo'dhyāyaḥ ślokaḥ 6

Om-Tat-Sat—Om (Braham) is the sole Reality. In the Yogic Scripture on the Science-of-Braham, the Shrimada-Bhāgvada-Gītā Upanishad, we hereby conclude Shloka 6 of the Dialogue between Shrī Krishna and Arjuna entitled Sanyāsa-Yoga, Canto V.

— ॐ अनन्ताय नमः ॐ —

Run Away to the Jungle? Really?

O my mind, why this fleeing haste—
This longing to cast off—and from this world walk away?
You dream of Vairagya – stillness in ochre robe and cave –
Yet still are unfree in mind, nor calm, nor brave!
You outwardly spurn deeds, yet still have many desires,
Which stay flickering within—like so many hidden fires!

Thou sayest, "Let me from the world retire, withdraw,"
But thy heart still trembles—confronted with inescapable worldly laws!
Hunger inevitably returns daily—demanding food be put in belly!
O mind, this flight from world is not freedom or release –
Ye still have yet to learn: How to first walk in peace.

O my soul, Lord Bhagwāna Shri Krishna has shown thee the way –
Not to flee but to walk—on the path of dharma & duty –
Which dharma for thee he has already out laid:

To serve Dharma with thy deeds, not with selfishness & greed,
To act in the cause of Sanatana-Dharma, casting aside thy own needs.
– Aye, this is the path which Shri Krishna has blessed –
The path of Karma-Yoga born of selflessness.

Thou needst not shun any work, rather to consecrate it –
And thusly transcend thy fate, the ego, this hunger, these bondages.
Aye, wean off all natural hunger—performing thy ordained dharma.
And through the sacred Varna-Ashram Dharma rightly performed,
Thou shall one day meet Bhagwana Shri Krishna—the All-in-One.

But alas, the Farce stays Operating

Renunciation for most is just an escape—
a name recited, a robe—white, yellow, ochre—an ashram, a cave,
The wild fire within—the fool, never didst tame.

ॐ गीता श्लोकः ५.७ – GĪTĀ VERSE 5.7

ॐ श्रीमद्भगवद्गीतासूपनिषत्सु ब्रह्मविद्यायां योगशास्त्रे श्रीकृष्णार्जुनसंवादे
om śrīmadbhagavadgītāsūpaniṣatsu brahmavidyāyāṁ yogaśāstre śrīkṛṣṇārjunasaṁvāde
संन्यासयोगो नाम पञ्चमोऽध्यायः श्लोकः ७
saṁnyāsayogo nāma pañcamo'dhyāyaḥ ślokaḥ 7

— ॐ —

योगयुक्तो विशुद्धात्मा विजितात्मा जितेन्द्रियः ।
yogayukto viśuddhātmā vijitātmā jitendriyaḥ
सर्वभूतात्मभूतात्मा कुर्वन्नपि न लिप्यते ॥५-७॥
sarvabhūtātmabhūtātmā kurvannapi na lipyate (5-7)

The Karma-Yogī—who has conquered the mind and mastered the senses, whose heart is pure, who has identified one's Self with the Self of all—remains untainted even though fully engaged in work. (5.7)

—: Word-by-Word :—

योगयुक्तः yogayuktaḥ – engaged in yoga; विशुद्धात्मा viśuddhātmā – pure in mind; विजितात्मा vijitātmā – self-controlled; जितेन्द्रियः jitendriyaḥ – having conquered the senses; सर्वभूतात्मभूतात्मा sarvabhūtātmabhūtātmā – seeing the Self in all beings; कुर्वन् kurvan – performing actions; अपि api – even; न na – not; लिप्यते lipyate – is tainted.

—: Understanding The Verse :—

— ॐ श्रीकृष्णाय नमः ॐ —

In this verse, Bhagwāna Shri Krishna offers a very luminous description of the one who is firmly established in Karma-Yoga.

The Lord delineates the characteristics of such a being: a purified mind, a self brought under mastery, the senses subdued, and the inner identification with the Self of all beings. Such a Yogi, though fully engaged in action, remains untainted, like the lotus untouched by the waters in which it dwells.

This verse marks a transition from merely affirming the equivalence of the paths of Knowledge and Action, to illustrating the inner state of the realized Karma-Yogī.

It conveys the central truth of the Gītā: that freedom lies not in abandoning action, but in transcending attachment to action. The Yoga-bound sage, though acting outwardly, is inwardly free, ever abiding in the Self—which is one within the Supreme-Self.

—: Key Sanskrit Terms :—

Let us open the verse gently, examining its essential Sanskrit terms to uncover the deeper layers woven within. Let us linger with the words like with a clear pool in mountain shadow. The disciplined yogi, pure, self-controlled, sees the same Self in all beings. Each syllable here reflects equality, the calm of vision undisturbed.

— ॐ —

योगयुक्तः (Yogayuktaḥ):

The योगयुक्तः yogayuktaḥ is the one firmly united with the spirit of Yoga — the fusion of inner detachment with outer engagement.

Such a soul acts not from compulsion but from divine harmony, where every deed becomes a silent offering to the Infinite.

— ॐ —

विशुद्धात्मा (Viśuddhātmā):

विशुद्धात्मा Viśuddhātmā — "one of purified self" — implies a heart free from the taints of selfish desire, pride, and fear.

Purity शुद्धि (śuddhi) here is not mere moral cleanness but the crystalline transparency of consciousness, where no shadow of ego dims the light of the Self.

— ॐ —

विजितात्मा (Vijitātmā) and जितेन्द्रियः (Jitendriyaḥ):

विजितात्मा Vijitātmā is one who has conquered the lower mind — the flickering desires and restless movements.

जितेन्द्रियः Jitendriyaḥ is he who has mastered the senses, no longer driven by the cries of sight, sound, taste, touch, and smell.

These victories are not through violence but through deep understanding and luminous discipline.

— ॐ —

सर्वभूतात्मभूतात्मा (Sarvabhūtātmabhūtātmā):

The soul who has realized his oneness with the Self of all beings — seeing no separation, no division.

He perceives the same luminous essence (Ātmā) shining in every creature, high or low, animate or inanimate.

— ॐ —

कुर्वन् अपि न लिप्यते (Kurvann api na lipyate):

Though such a soul acts कुर्वन् (kurvan), he is न लिप्यते na lipyate — untouched, unstained by action.

His deeds, free from desire and ego, leave no imprint upon him, just as a lotus remains dry though born amidst water.

Lo, each phrase of this verse reveals the portrait of the perfected Karma-Yogī — a living embodiment of purity, mastery, universality, inner freedom.

—: *In Brief* :—

— ॐ श्रीकृष्णाय नमः ॐ —

Bhagwāna Shri Krishna, continuing His glorification of Karma-Yoga, now reveals the inner condition of the perfected Karma-Yogī.

Such a one is described through a constellation of noble qualities:
योगयुक्त Yoga-yuktaḥ—united with Yoga;
विशुद्धात्मा viśuddhātmā—of purified inner being;
विजितात्मा vijitātmā—self-conquered;
जितेन्द्रियः jitendriyaḥ—master of the senses;
and most strikingly: सर्वभूतात्मभूतात्मा sarva-bhūta-ātma-bhūta-ātmā—whose very Self has become the Self of all beings.

— ॐ श्रीरामाय नमः ॐ —

This profound expression means that such a sage no longer sees himself as a separate little 'I', but as the one universal Self that dwells in all creation.

He does not merely believe this philosophically—he lives it existentially. In him, the veil of individuality has fallen, and he perceives only the One—expressing Himself through the many.

— ॐ महाधनुष्मते नमः ॐ —

Though this Yogi acts in the world, he remains untainted by action. His actions do not spring from selfish desire, nor are they governed by the fluctuations of pleasure and pain.

Like the sun, which shines upon all without attachment, or the lotus, which remains untouched by the water in which it grows, such a कर्म-योगी Karma-Yogī is inwardly untouched by the results of his deeds.

This purity is not merely moral, but ontological—the result of identification with the Divine, the Supreme Self that is beyond all change and unaffected by karma.

Because he sees all beings as manifestations of the same Braham, there is no selfish motive, no partiality, no fear, no pride.

In such a one, doership dissolves.

— ॐ रामभद्राय नमः ॐ —

The phrase "सर्वभूतात्मभूतात्मा sarva-bhūta-ātma-bhūta-ātmā" may also be interpreted to mean: "He whose Self has become the Self of all beings, and for whom all beings have become his very own Self."

This indicates not only non-dual realization, but also a spontaneous compassion and universal love for all existence—born of the Jnana that all is the oneness of Braham. He seeks the welfare of all beings—and not just humans—for he sees them as not the "other".

Such a state is not attained through intellectual understanding alone, nor by dry ascetic renunciation that's void of surrender to the one consciousness that pervades throughout. It is the very fruit of कर्म-योग Karma-Yoga—when practiced with unwavering devotion, discrimination, and detachment.

In earlier verses, Shri Krishna explained that even a little of this Yoga protects one from great fear. Here, He shows that when perfected, it makes one like unto Braham—actionless in the midst of action, silent amidst speech, at rest amidst motion.

— ॐ वासुदेवाय नमः ॐ —

The marvel is this: the साङ्ख्ययोगी Sānkhya-Yogī, the contemplative sage, does not consider himself the doer at all. But even the कर्म-योगी Karma-Yogī, who appears as a doer and engages in action, if acting in the spirit of surrender to the Divine, remains equally unbound.

This is the supreme mystery of कर्म-योग Karma-Yoga—to act without acting, to do without doership.

Thus, the कर्म-योगी Karma-Yogī, even though engaged in all the affairs of life, lives as one who is free. He is untouched by karma because he is untouched by ego. The fruit of his discipline is not mere outer success, but union with the Supreme Self, and the capacity to serve the world without ever becoming enslaved by it.

In the verses that follow, Shri Krishna will further explore how this vision of oneness with all beings becomes the basis of equanimity, peace, and true wisdom, leading the Yogi into ever-deeper intimacy with the Infinite.

— ॐ तत सत ॐ —

Before we move on, let us bow in reverence to this sacred verse. Write it by hand, reflect on its meaning, chant it aloud, make it your own.

— ॐ —

योगयुक्तो विशुद्धात्मा विजितात्मा जितेन्द्रियः ।
yogayukto viśuddhātmā vijitātmā jitendriyaḥ
सर्वभूतात्मभूतात्मा कुर्वन्नपि न लिप्यते ॥५-७॥
sarvabhūtātmabhūtātmā kurvannapi na lipyate (5-7)

ॐ

योगयुक्तो विशुद्धात्मा विजितात्मा जितेन्द्रियः ।
yogayukto viśuddhātmā vijitātmā jitendriyaḥ
सर्वभूतात्मभूतात्मा कुर्वन्नपि न लिप्यते ॥५-७॥
sarvabhūtātmabhūtātmā kurvannapi na lipyate (5-7)

ॐ तत्सदिति श्रीमद्भगवद्गीतासूपनिषत्सु ब्रह्मविद्यायां योगशास्त्रे श्रीकृष्णार्जुनसंवादे
om tatsaditi śrīmadbhagavadgītāsūpaniṣatsu brahmavidyāyāṁ yogaśāstre śrīkṛṣṇārjunasaṁvāde
संन्यासयोगो नाम पञ्चमोऽध्यायः श्लोकः ७
saṁnyāsayogo nāma pañcamo'dhyāyaḥ ślokaḥ 7

Om-Tat-Sat—Om (Braham) is the sole Reality. In the Yogic Scripture on the Science-of-Braham, the Shrimada-Bhāgvada-Gītā Upanishad, we hereby conclude Shloka 7 of the Dialogue between Shrī Krishna and Arjuna entitled Sanyāsa-Yoga, Canto V.

— ॐ करुणाकराय नमः ॐ —

The Ocean Beneath the Rising Waves

The sea may roar in foam and wave,
may crash in wrath or gleam with light,
Yet far beneath its heaving skin—
abides a calm beyond all earthly heaps;
And that is the Self which the Yogi knows himself as!

Though waves of karma around him rise,
Yet, untouched by toil, unmoved by cries,
His soul abides deep as the changeless sky.

He walks midst men, doing deeds of men,
yet bears no burden upon his breath—
Because he knows himself to be that shoreless Sea,
where work is naught -- and there's no more death.

The Self is One, and everything is That—
no wave can mar that Ocean Infinite.
The Karma-Yogi acts, yet ever rests in Him,
Where all forms dissolve, and there exists no division.

He Is The True King

The Karma-Yogi has conquered—
not kingdoms, but his mind.
He has won over—not crowds, but cravings.
Ruled by none, he rules no one—
and thus is King.

ॐ गीता श्लोकः ५.८-९ – Gītā Verse 5.8-9

ॐ श्रीमद्भगवद्गीतासूपनिषत्सु ब्रह्मविद्यायां योगशास्त्रे श्रीकृष्णार्जुनसंवादे
om śrīmadbhagavadgītāsūpaniṣatsu brahmavidyāyāṁ yogaśāstre śrīkṛṣṇārjunasaṁvāde
संन्यासयोगो नाम पञ्चमोऽध्यायः श्लोकः ८-९
saṁnyāsayogo nāma pañcamo'dhyāyaḥ ślokaḥ 8-9

— ॐ —

नैव किञ्चित्करोमीति युक्तो मन्येत तत्त्ववित् ।
naiva kiñcitkaromīti yukto manyeta tattvavit
पश्यञ्शृण्वन्स्पृशञ्जिघ्रन्नश्नन्गच्छन्स्वपञ्श्वसन् ॥५-८॥
paśyañśṛṇvanspṛśañjighrannaśnangacchansvapañśvasan (5-8)

प्रलपन्विसृजन्गृह्णन्नुन्मिषन्निमिषन्नपि ।
pralapanvisṛjangṛhṇannunmiṣannimiṣannapi
इन्द्रियाणीन्द्रियार्थेषु वर्तन्त इति धारयन् ॥५-९॥
indriyāṇīndriyārtheṣu vartanta iti dhārayan (5-9)

The Yogī who knows the nature of reality, ever avers, 'I am not the doer'—even though seeing, hearing, touching, smelling, feeding, walking, sleeping, breathing, speaking, excreting, grasping, blinking etc.,—maintaining that it is the sense-organs alone, moving amidst the sense-objects, which react and enact. (5.8-5.9)

—: Word-by-Word :—

न na – not; एव eva – indeed; किञ्चित् kiñcit – anything; करोमि karomi – do I do; इति iti – thus; युक्तः yuktaḥ – united in yoga; मन्येत manyeta – should think; तत्त्ववित् tattvavit – the knower of truth; पश्यन् paśyan – seeing; शृण्वन् śṛṇvan – hearing; स्पृशन् spṛśan – touching; जिघ्रन् jighran – smelling; अश्नन् aśnan – eating; गच्छन् gacchan – going; स्वपन् svapan – sleeping; श्वसन् śvasan – breathing.

प्रलपन् pralapan – speaking; विसृजन् visṛjan – abandoning; गृह्णन् gṛhṇan – accepting; उन्मिषन् unmiṣan – opening (the eyes); निमिषन् nimiṣan – closing (the eyes); अपि api – even; इन्द्रियाणि indriyāṇi – the senses; इन्द्रियार्थेषु indriya-artheṣu – among the sense objects; वर्तन्त vartanta – act; इति iti – thus; धारयन् dhārayan – holding (in understanding).

—: Understanding The Verse :—

— ॐ श्रीकृष्णाय नमः ॐ —

In these verses, Bhagwāna Shri Krishna unveils the inner vision of the realized Yogi—the one who, having attained true Knowledge, no longer identifies himself as the doer of karmas.

Though the body continues to act—seeing, hearing, walking, speaking, sleeping, breathing, eating, and so forth—the enlightened one remains inwardly untouched, abiding just in the Self, staying fully free.

Shri Krishna affirms that such a knower of the Truth तत्त्ववित (tattva-vit) recognizes all activities to be the movements of guṇas of nature, working through the sense-organs, which themselves are but modifications of प्रकृति Prakṛti.

— ॐ श्रीरामाय नमः ॐ —

The तत्त्ववित् tattva-vit perceives the Self as actionless and unchanging, a witness साक्षी (sākṣin) to all phenomena, and thereby remains untainted by action, like the sky remains unstained by the clouds that drift across it.

These verses thus deepen the teaching of Karma-Yoga and non-doership अकर्तृत्वम् (akartṛtvam) by presenting the lived-perception of the liberated sage. It is not renunciation of action—rather renunciation of identification with action, and which leads to liberation.

—: Key Sanskrit Terms :—

Let us reflect on the verses' key Sanskrit terms, each of which is like a thread that weaves into the verse's deeper fabric of meaning. Each words rest here as like a yogi walking through the marketplace, moving yet unmoved; eating, walking, sleeping, speaking—he knows "I do nothing." Each word empties the act of ego, leaving only presence.

— ॐ —

युक्तः तत्त्ववित् (Yuktaḥ Tattvavit):

The युक्तः yuktaḥ — the one steadfast in Yoga, and the तत्त्ववित् tattvavit — the knower of Reality - these are not two, but one luminous being.

The तत्त्ववित् Tattvavit is indicative of direct realization अपरोक्ष -ज्ञान (aparokṣa-jñāna) of the Self as actionless, immutable, untouched by the movements of प्रकृति prakṛti.

Such a one is united with the Supreme not by mere discipline, but by knowledge born of direct seeing.

— ॐ —

नैव किञ्चित्करोमि इति (Naiva kiñcit karomi iti): "I do nothing at all" — not a denial of apparent activity, but the deep, silent understanding that the Self, being pure Awareness, is beyond the play of actions.

The yogi sees that all motion belongs to the body, mind, and senses — mere instruments animated by प्रकृति prakṛti — while the Self remains the unchanging witness.

— ॐ —

पश्यन्, शृण्वन्, स्पृशन्, जिघ्रन्, अश्नन्... (Paśyan, Śṛṇvan, Spṛśan, Jighran, Aśnan...): A flowing list of mundane actions — seeing, hearing, touching, smelling, eating, moving, sleeping, breathing. These are the natural functions of the body-sense complex. They are presented not as errors, but as natural phenomena, harmless when the false notion of "I am the doer" कर्तृत्व-अभिमान (kartṛtva-abhimāna) is absent.

— ॐ —

इन्द्रियाणि इन्द्रियार्थेषु वर्तन्ते (Indriyāṇi indriyārtheṣu vartante): "The senses move among the sense-objects" — this profound vision dissolves the imagined ownership of action.

Just as rivers flow into the ocean without affecting its vastness, so too the movements of the senses leave the Self untouched.

The sage sees action happening within प्रकृति prakṛti, while he himself, as pure awareness, remains ever free.

— ॐ —

धारयन् Dhārayan — holding this realization firm, sustaining it as the very foundation of his perception.

Not a fleeting glimpse, but an unshakable abiding in Truth.

Each phrase here weaves a seamless tapestry of the liberated vision: acting yet not acting, moving yet unmoving, living as the silent witness amid the ceaseless dance of existence.

—: In Brief :—

— ॐ श्रीकृष्णाय नमः ॐ —

Here, Bhagwāna Shri Krishna opens a window into the sublime vision of the true साङ्ख्ययोगी Sankhya-Yogī, the knower of Reality तत्त्ववित् (tattva-vit), who abides in unwavering identity with the Self आत्मा (Ātmā).

Though the body is engaged in a multitude of activities—perceiving the world, moving, speaking, breathing, sleeping, and more—the realized Yogi remains inwardly untouched, ever asserting: "न एव किञ्चित् करोमि na eva kiñcit karomi"—"I do nothing at all."

This is not the utterance of negligence or delusion, but the calm declaration of one who has awakened to the truth that the Self is actionless—अकर्ता akartā, the eternal witness of all movements, untouched by the functions of body, mind, or senses.

— ॐ श्रीरामाय नमः ॐ —

The enumeration of actions—seeing, hearing, touching, eating, walking, excreting, speaking, grasping, opening and closing the eyes—serves a profound purpose. These acts encompass the full range of sensory and motor functions, as well as the workings of the inner faculties. And yet, the Yogi sees that it is not "I" who acts, but merely the senses engaging with the sense-objects, प्रकृति Prakṛti moving within प्रकृति Prakṛti, governed by the laws of the three गुण guṇas.

This discernment dissolves the sense of doership अहंकार (ahaṅkāra), the root of bondage.

— ॐ श्रीसीतामनोरमाय नमः ॐ —

As long as one believes, "I see, I eat, I speak," the ego is affirmed, and karma accrues. But when one clearly perceives that all functions arise from the interplay of nature, with the Self remaining aloof and changeless, karmas no longer bind.

This is the wisdom of साङ्ख्य Sankhya: to realize that the Self neither acts nor is acted upon.

— ॐ विष्णवे नमः ॐ —

सर्वथा वर्तमानोऽपि sarvathā vartamāno'pi—even though engaged in all manner of activities, I can still remain disengaged. It affirms that liberation is not conditioned by external inactivity.

One may walk, speak, sleep, or act in the world, and yet remain utterly free, provided there is no inner identification with the act. This is the Gītā's revolutionary teaching: one may live in the world and yet be not be of the world.

— ॐ मुकुन्दाय नमः ॐ —

Such a Yogi sees the entire phenomenal world as a passing show, a play of appearances projected upon the substratum of Braham. For him, likes and dislikes, longing and aversion, have lost their grip. He moves through the world as one in a dream—not deceived by it, nor bound by it.

It is also notable how these verses mirror other teachings of the Gītā:

"गुणा गुणेषु वर्तन्त Guṇāḥ guṇeṣu vartante" (3.28): "The guṇas move among the guṇas."

"प्रकृतेः क्रियमाणानि...सर्वशः Prakṛtiḥ kriyamāṇāni...sarvaśaḥ" (3.27): "All actions are performed by Prakṛti."

These are not merely philosophical doctrines but the experiential realization of the one who has known and now truly sees.

— ॐ पुण्योदयाय नमः ॐ —

Indeed, the साङ्ख्ययोगी Sankhya-Yogī, having destroyed the seed of ego and desire, may perform any action that accords with his station and dharma—teaching, speaking, eating, resting—without accruing bondage. His mind is like a still lake, unmoved by ripples; his life is like a flute, hollow yet resonant with the Divine breath.

These verses offer not merely instruction, but a portrait of the liberated being, whose life is a living यज्ञ Yajña, whose actions are non-actions, whose presence sanctifies the world, even while he walks unnoticed among men.

In the verses to follow, Bhagwāna Shri Krishna will reveal how such a Yogi, abiding in equanimity and Self-awareness, remains untouched by karma as a lotus leaf by water, pointing to the profound inner freedom that lies at the heart of all true Yoga.

— ॐ तत सत ॐ —

Before we move on, let us bow in reverence to this sacred verse. Write it by hand, reflect on its meaning, chant it aloud, make it your own.

— ॐ —

नैव किञ्चित्करोमीति युक्तो मन्येत तत्त्ववित् ।
naiva kiñcitkaromīti yukto manyeta tattvavit
पश्यञ्शृण्वन्स्पृशञ्जिघ्रन्नश्नन्गच्छन्स्वपञ्श्वसन् ॥५-८॥
paśyañśṛṇvanspṛśañjighrannaśnangacchansvapañśvasan (5-8)

प्रलपन्विसृजन्गृह्णन्नुन्मिषन्निमिषन्नपि ।
pralapanvisṛjangṛhṇannunmiṣannimiṣannapi
इन्द्रियाणीन्द्रियार्थेषु वर्तन्त इति धारयन् ॥५-९॥
indriyāṇīndriyārtheṣu vartanta iti dhārayan (5-9)

— ॐ —

नैव किञ्चित्करोमीति युक्तो मन्येत तत्त्ववित् ।
naiva kiñcitkaromīti yukto manyeta tattvavit
पश्यञ्शृण्वन्स्पृशञ्जिघ्रन्नश्नन्गच्छन्स्वपञ्श्वसन् ॥५-८॥
paśyañśṛṇvanspṛśañjighrannaśnangacchansvapañśvasan (5-8)

प्रलपन्विसृजन्गृह्णन्नुन्मिषन्निमिषन्नपि ।
pralapanvisṛjangṛhṇannunmiṣannimiṣannapi
इन्द्रियाणीन्द्रियार्थेषु वर्तन्त इति धारयन् ॥५-९॥
indriyāṇīndriyārtheṣu vartanta iti dhārayan (5-9)

ॐ तत्सदिति श्रीमद्भगवद्गीतासूपनिषत्सु ब्रह्मविद्यायां योगशास्त्रे श्रीकृष्णार्जुनसंवादे
om tatsaditi śrīmadbhagavadgītāsūpaniṣatsu brahmavidyāyāṁ yogaśāstre śrīkṛṣṇārjunasaṁvāde
संन्यासयोगो नाम पञ्चमोऽध्यायः श्लोकः ८-९
saṁnyāsayogo nāma pañcamo'dhyāyaḥ ślokaḥ 8-9

Om-Tat-Sat—Om (Braham) is the sole Reality. In the Yogic Scripture on the Science-of-Braham, the Shrimada-Bhāgvada-Gītā Upanishad, we hereby conclude Shloka 8-9 of the Dialogue between Shrī Krishna and Arjuna entitled Sanyāsa-Yoga, Canto V.

— ॐ श्रीकृष्णाय नमः ॐ —

Ah, this Verse Strikes Like a Bell — in a Temple Long-Abandoned

"I am not the doer," says the knower.
Though eyes see, though breath breathes,
though hands reach—he remains untouched.
The body acts,
Yet the Self abides aloof, unconcerned.

I am the Sky That Watches All, Yet I stay Unmoved, Unstirred

The clouds may gather—golden, or grey, or grim,
And winds may howl—or stay hushed in twilight dim,
Yet the sky remains, untouched—unmoved, unbent, free, serene,
A dome of stillness o'er the changing sea.

And such is the Self, the ātmā, the "I"— within the Yogi's gaze—
Unmoved by the senses,
unshaken, unafraid of sense's eagerness—
of the senses tantrums—of their glowering, threatening demeanor.

The Yogi knows: This Here is Not My Home.

Though eyes may weep, and feet onward roam,
The Karma-Yogi knows the great Gita Truth:
"It is only Nature acting, reacting,
performing in its natural course.
I Act not. I am not the Doer.
And this here—is not my Home."

The Karma-Yogi watches all,
Maybe living in a shack, or perhaps ruling empires and kingdoms,
But always the sovereign of a different Realm he remains—supernal,
claiming none and nothing of earth to be his own.

ॐ गीता श्लोकः ५.१० – GĪTĀ VERSE 5.10

ॐ श्रीमद्भगवद्गीतासूपनिषत्सु ब्रह्मविद्यायां योगशास्त्रे श्रीकृष्णार्जुनसंवादे
om śrīmadbhagavadgītāsūpaniṣatsu brahmavidyāyāṁ yogaśāstre śrīkṛṣṇārjunasaṁvāde
संन्यासयोगो नाम पञ्चमोऽध्यायः श्लोकः १०
saṁnyāsayogo nāma pañcamo'dhyāyaḥ ślokaḥ 10

— ॐ —

ब्रह्मण्याधाय कर्माणि सङ्गं त्यक्त्वा करोति यः ।
brahmaṇyādhāya karmāṇi saṅgaṁ tyaktvā karoti yaḥ
लिप्यते न स पापेन पद्मपत्रमिवाम्भसा ॥५-१०॥
lipyate na sa pāpena padmapatramivāmbhasā (5-10)

One who, giving up attachment, performs all actions dedicating them unto the Lord, always remains untainted by sin—in the same way as the lotus-leaf remains untouched by water. (5.10)

—: Word-by-Word :—

ब्रह्मणि brahmaṇi – in Brahman; **आधाय** ādhāya – placing; **कर्माणि** karmāṇi – actions; **सङ्गं** saṅgam – attachment; **त्यक्त्वा** tyaktvā – having abandoned; **करोति** yaḥ – who performs; **लिप्यते** na – is not tainted; **सः** saḥ – he; **पापेन** pāpena – by sin; **पद्मपत्रम्** padmapatram – like a lotus leaf; **इव** iva – as; **अम्भसा** ambhasā – by water.

—: Understanding The Verse :—

— ॐ श्रीकृष्णाय नमः ॐ —

In this verse, Bhagwāna Shri Krishna deepens the teaching of Karma-Yoga by illustrating the inner attitude with which all actions must be performed. He declares that one who, abandoning all attachment, performs every act as an offering unto the Supreme (Braham), remains untainted by sin, just as the lotus leaf remains untouched by water, though it rests upon it and in it grows.

This verse emphasizes the secret of inner freedom amidst outer activity. It is not action that binds, but the sense of possessiveness and ego—the idea of "I do" and "this is mine".

When actions are performed with the spirit of surrender, offering them to the Divine without craving for results, such acts no longer generate bondage. The Yogi remains inwardly unstained, like the lotus in the lake.

—: Key Sanskrit Terms :—

Let us begin our exploration of the verse by pausing at each of the terms through which its deeper purpose will gradually emerge. Let us hear the Sanskrit words—that are alike the lotus floating untouched by water. He who acts without clinging, offering all to Braham, remains untainted. Each syllable is a petal unstained—serene upon the floodplain of a chaotic world.

— ॐ —

ब्रह्मणि आधाय कर्माणि (Brahmaṇy ādhāya karmāṇi):

Here, ब्रह्मणि आधाय brahmaṇi ādhāya — "offering actions to Braham" — is the profound practice of surrendering every deed into the vastness of the Supreme.

Actions are no longer performed with the fever of personal desire, but are consecrated as offerings at the feet of the Infinite. The doer is erased; only worship remains.

— ॐ —

सङ्गं त्यक्त्वा (Saṅgaṁ tyaktvā):

- सङ्गं Saṅga — attachment, clinging to outcomes, to success or failure—is the subtle thread that binds the soul to action's consequences.

- त्यक्त्वा Tyaktvā, the abandonment of this attachment, is the true severance of bondage.

Without सङ्गं saṅga, action becomes a pure flow, devoid of entanglement.

— ॐ —

लिप्यते न (Lipyate na):

लिप्यते Lipyate — "is stained" — indicates the soul's freedom from the karmic residue of deeds.

Actions leave no trace upon the purified consciousness; the soul remains immaculate, like the sky untouched by passing clouds.

— ॐ —

पद्मपत्रम् इव अम्भसा (Padmapatram iva ambhasā):

The imagery is exquisite: just as the lotus-leaf पद्मपत्रम् (padmapatram) remains untouched by the waters अम्भसा (ambhasā) that surround it, so too the realized being lives amidst the waters of worldly action yet remains ever dry, ever pure, ever free.

The lotus, rooted in mud yet blooming pristine, becomes the living symbol of spiritual perfection.

Each word of this lovely verse unveils the secret of living in the world without being of the world — moving amidst action yet abiding in an inner stillness.

—: In Brief :—

— ॐ श्रीकृष्णाय नमः ॐ —

In this sublime verse, Bhagwāna Shri Krishna reveals the essence of purified action: that true Karma-Yoga lies not in the action itself, but in the motive and dedication behind it.

The Yogi who abandons all attachment, and performs actions offering them unto Braham, remains inwardly untouched—अलिप्य alipta, asamliṅgaḥ, unentangled, unblemished—by even the possibility of sin.

— ॐ श्रीरामाय नमः ॐ —

The phrase "ब्रह्मण्याधाय कर्माणि brahmaṇi ādhāya karmāṇi" is of immense spiritual significance. It means to consecrate all actions unto Braham, the Supreme Reality—whose manifest presence on earth is in the shape of Krishna.

This is not mere ritualism, but a transformation of consciousness. The Yogi sees every act—not just worship or austerity, but the simplest deeds of daily life—as a sacred offering. Whether eating, speaking, walking, or working, all is surrendered unto the Supreme.

Because of this, the Yogi's actions no longer arise from self-will or desire, but from obedience to his duties that have been ordained for him by dint of his वर्ण-आश्रम-धर्म Varna-Āshrama dharma; and staying in full surrender to Krishna and Sanātana-Dharma, he keeps his heart open for divine prompting.

Verily he becomes an instrument in the hands of the Divine, like a flute that produces music when the breath of the Lord passes through it.

— ॐ श्रीरामाय नमः ॐ —

The metaphor of the lotus leaf पद्मपत्र इव (padma-patram iva) is exquisitely chosen. The lotus grows in muddy waters, yet remains unstained. Likewise, the Karma-Yogī moves amidst the world of duality and action, but remains inwardly pure, unaffected by the world's contaminations.

Just as water may fall on the lotus-leaf but cannot cling to it, so too do the fruits of karma roll off the Yogi's inner being without leaving any traces.

This detachment is not born of indifference, but of deep surrender. The Yogi acts not out of selfish impulse, but out of alignment with the will of the Divine.

He does not act for pleasure, gain, recognition, or even personal virtue.

He acts because it is his duty, and he offers all outcomes at the feet of Lord-God Bhagwāna Shri Krishna.

— ॐ रासविलासिनाय नमः ॐ —

The word **पाप** pāpa (sin) in this context refers not merely to transgressive acts, but to anything that binds the soul—attachments, egoism, and the lingering sense of doership.

The Yogi, by surrendering action, becomes free of such residues. His very life becomes a yajña, a sacred sacrifice.

It is also important to note that this inner purity is not confined to certain prescribed actions. Even ordinary acts—eating, walking, speaking—when done without attachment and as an offering to the Supreme, become sacred.

The Lord teaches here that purity does not lie in what one does, but in how and why one does it.

— ॐ धन्विने नमः ॐ —

Through this teaching, Shri Krishna exalts the life of inner renunciation over outer withdrawal.

The **कर्म-योगी** Karma-Yogī need not renounce the world; he need only renounce attachment, ego, and expectation. When he does so, the world can no longer bind him.

In the next verses, Bhagwāna will continue to describe the state of such a purified Yogi, who, through performance of ordained-karma and inner detachment, becomes ever absorbed in the Self, and at peace in the midst of all activity.

— ॐ तत सत ॐ —

Before we move on, let us bow in reverence to this sacred verse. Write it by hand, reflect on its meaning, chant it aloud, make it your own.

— ॐ —

ब्रह्मण्याधाय कर्माणि सङ्गं त्यक्त्वा करोति यः ।
brahmaṇyādhāya karmāṇi saṅgaṁ tyaktvā karoti yaḥ
लिप्यते न स पापेन पद्मपत्रमिवाम्भसा ॥५-१०॥
lipyate na sa pāpena padmapatramivāmbhasā (5-10)

— ॐ —

ब्रह्मण्याधाय कर्माणि सङ्गं त्यक्त्वा करोति यः ।
brahmaṇyādhāya karmāṇi saṅgaṁ tyaktvā karoti yaḥ

लिप्यते न स पापेन पद्मपत्रमिवाम्भसा ॥५-१०॥
lipyate na sa pāpena padmapatramivāmbhasā (5-10)

ॐ तत्सदिति श्रीमद्भगवद्गीतासूपनिषत्सु ब्रह्मविद्यायां योगशास्त्रे श्रीकृष्णार्जुनसंवादे
om tatsaditi śrīmadbhagavadgītāsūpaniṣatsu brahmavidyāyāṁ yogaśāstre śrīkṛṣṇārjunasaṁvāde
संन्यासयोगो नाम पञ्चमोऽध्यायः श्लोकः १०
saṁnyāsayogo nāma pañcamo'dhyāyaḥ ślokaḥ 10

Om-Tat-Sat—Om (Braham) is the sole Reality. In the Yogic Scripture on the Science-of-Braham, the Shrimada-Bhāgvada-Gītā Upanishad, we hereby conclude Shloka 10 of the Dialogue between Shrī Krishna and Arjuna entitled Sanyāsa-Yoga, Canto V.

— ॐ श्रीकृष्णगोविंदाय नमः ॐ —

Torn In Twain

O me, how oft I stumble blind,
Tossed between the silence and the grind.
If freedom lies in dropping deeds,
Then why doth the Lord still urge to do & lead?
Why bid me stay where sorrows grow,
And not to flee to where silence flows?
My hands are stained with earthly toil,
Yet my soul would rather shun this mortal soil.
O heart, how shall I break this knot,
And know what's true and what false?

Two Paths, One Sun

O weary soul, thy Lord hath spoken,
And with His words in Gita thy doubt stands broken.
He weaveth not two ways, but one —
A path of gold beneath the sun.
Renounce within, but outwardly serve —
Let not the motion of these outer steps, thee unnerve.

The yogi walks in the world—hands working, open eyes,
But to him just Atman and Dharma alone stay sterling & high.
With duty/dharma done, the soul is set free,
The path of Karma-Yoga thus becomes the gateway to liberty.

The wise Do Not Stay Divided.

They walk the one Sanātana path of Karma—which may have many names.
They dwell in bliss—even through hectic work, stay in that stillness,
Just one breath flows through both the course.
Sankhya or karma, the same flame burns underneath both.

ॐ गीता श्लोकः ५.११ – GĪTĀ VERSE 5.11

ॐ श्रीमद्भगवद्गीतासूपनिषत्सु ब्रह्मविद्यायां योगशास्त्रे श्रीकृष्णार्जुनसंवादे
om śrīmadbhagavadgītāsūpaniṣatsu brahmavidyāyāṁ yogaśāstre śrīkṛṣṇārjunasaṁvāde
संन्यासयोगो नाम पञ्चमोऽध्यायः श्लोकः ११
saṁnyāsayogo nāma pañcamo'dhyāyaḥ ślokaḥ 11

— ॐ —

कायेन मनसा बुद्ध्या केवलैरिन्द्रियैरपि ।
kāyena manasā buddhyā kevalairindriyairapi
योगिनः कर्म कुर्वन्ति सङ्गं त्यक्त्वात्मशुद्धये ॥५-११॥
yoginaḥ karma kurvanti saṅgaṁ tyaktvātmaśuddhaye (5-11)

Completely giving up attachments, the Karma-Yogī simply carries out duties—through the instrument of the body, mind, intellect and organs—only with a view towards self-purification. (5.11)

—: Word-by-Word :—

कायेन kāyena – with the body; मनसा manasā – with the mind; बुद्ध्या buddhyā – with the intellect; केवलैः kevalaiḥ – with pure; इन्द्रियैः indriyaiḥ – senses; अपि api – even; योगिनः yoginaḥ – yogis; कर्म karma – actions; कुर्वन्ति kurvanti – perform; सङ्गं tyaktvā – abandoning attachment; आत्मशुद्धये ātma-śuddhaye – for the purification of the self.

—: Understanding The Verse :—

— ॐ श्रीकृष्णाय नमः ॐ —

In this illumining verse, Bhagwāna Shri Krishna delineates the inner disposition and spiritual orientation of the Karma-Yogi—one who follows the noble path of performing ordained-karmas in line with one's वर्ण-आश्रम Varna-Āshrama.

Distinct from the one who acts out of worldly desires and deemed obligations, the Karma-Yogi undertakes all actions solely to serve Dharma, as an offering to Krishna—from whom has emerged सनातन-धर्म Sanātana-Dharma—devoid of possessiveness or craving for personal gain.

— ॐ श्रीरामाय नमः ॐ —

Shri Krishna affirms that such a seeker employs the काया kāya (body), मान्स manas (mind), बुद्धि buddhi (intellect), and इन्द्रिय indriyas (senses), as the instruments to perform his duties without clinging to the notion of "I" and "mine."

This self-effacing attitude is not one of passivity but of great inward clarity, for the Karma-Yogi's sole aim is the शुद्धि śuddhi—the purification—of the self so that the real Self shines through.

This verse thus explores the essence of निष्काम-कर्म niṣkāma-karma—action without desire—as a sacred discipline. It teaches that the performance of duty, when infused with detachment and dedicated to the higher goal of inner purification, becomes an instrument of liberation rather than bondage.

— ॐ भक्तवत्सलाय नमः ॐ —

O mortal, be the Actor who knows he is the soul and not the role.

Just as an actor plays his role convincingly but never mistakes himself for the character, the Karma-Yogī uses the body and senses without identifying with them.

O man, be that pen which writes without ownership of the story.

The body, mind, and intellect are like the pen; the Self is the writer shaping the story in line with the ancient script of Sanātana-Dharma.

The pen simply moves according to a divine script—which Krishna long ago decreed when He breathed into the world Sanātana-Dharma: the cosmic order by which all must live and by which alone is our survival possible.

—: Key Sanskrit Terms :—

Now let us bend close to the verse, like a listener to a conch's song, and now hearken to the resonances held within its Sanskrit voice—each word a portal to realms unseen, each word like a craftsman at his work. The Yogis act with body, mind, intellect, and senses—only for purification. Each word chisels away the crust of attachment, leaving clarity.

— ॐ —

कायेन मनसा बुद्ध्या (Kāyena manasā buddhyā):
The yogins act through the काया मानस बुद्धि kāya (body), manas (mind), and buddhi (intellect) — recognizing these as instruments उपाधि (upādhi), not as the Self.
The body moves, the mind thinks, the intellect discerns — yet the indwelling spirit remains ever the silent witness.

— ॐ —

केवलैः इन्द्रियैः अपि (Kevalaiḥ indriyaiḥ api):

केवलैः Kevalaiḥ — "merely," "alone" — emphasizes the mechanical functioning of the senses इन्द्रियाणि (indriyāṇi) in relation to their respective objects.

The योगी yogin perceives these activities as natural movements within प्रकृति prakṛti, devoid of any "I-ness" (ahamkāra).

— ॐ —

योगिनः कर्म कुर्वन्ति (Yoginaḥ karma kurvanti):

The योगिनः yoginaḥ — the true yogīs — continue to perform karma (action), but not as agents seeking fulfillment through action.

Their doing is free from the entanglements of desire, performed as part of the cosmic order ऋत (ṛta), not personal ambition.

— ॐ —

सङ्गं त्यक्त्वा (Saṅgaṁ tyaktvā):

सङ्ग Saṅga — the inner clinging to the fruits or outcomes of action — is wholly renounced.

The yogin acts with complete त्याग tyāga (abandonment), dedicating every act to the Divine, with no residue of personal craving.

— ॐ —

आत्मशुद्धये (Ātmaśuddhaye):

The purpose of action is now आत्म-शुद्धि ātmaśuddhi — the purification of the inner being. Action becomes a sacred fire in which the dross of ego, attachment, and ignorance is burned away.

Not action for reward, but action for the blossoming of the soul into its pristine, luminous nature.

O behold, see how every word in this verse breathes the quiet grandeur of life divine — a life where every movement becomes an instrument for inner purification and ascent up to the Eternal.

—: In Brief :—

— ॐ श्रीकृष्णाय नमः ॐ —

The Karma-Yogi, says Shri Krishna, performs all actions—whether mental, verbal, or physical—merely as a means of आत्म-शुद्धि ātma-śuddhi, inner purification.

The term केवलैः kevalaiḥ (merely, solely) in the verse underscores the utter absence of self-centered motives or the sense of doership.

Though the word directly qualifies इन्द्रियैः indriyaiḥ (by the senses), by implication, it extends to the काया kāya (body), मानस manas (mind), and बुद्धि buddhi (intellect) as well.

The Karma-Yogi harbors no possessive identity with any of these instruments; he sees them as belonging not to the ego but to Īśvara, the Supreme.

Such an individual acts not for the gratification of personal desire, nor for gain, praise, or recognition. Rather, he acts as निमित्तमात्र nimitta-mātra, a mere instrument in the hands of the Divine.

His mind, untainted by attachment, is a clear mirror that reflects the will of Bhagwāna. In this way, even while engaging in the world, the Karma-Yogi remains inwardly free.

— ॐ श्रीरामाय नमः ॐ —

This verse sets the stage for the next instruction, wherein Shri Krishna continues to unfold the qualities of the संन्यासी sannyāsī and योगी yogī, showing that it is not the mere renunciation of action but the renunciation of attachment that brings peace and freedom.

The path of योग Yoga is a path not away from the world, but through it—sanctified by wisdom and sustained by detachment.

— ॐ तत सत ॐ —

Before we move on, let us bow in reverence to this sacred verse—a timeless beacon of wisdom guiding seekers for ages. Write it by hand, reflect on its meaning, and chant it aloud, for these sounds alone carry the authenticity of that era. The world may have changed but the living vibration of these Sanskrit sounds still remain as original as they were when Bhagwān Shri Krishna Himself walked the earth and imparted these teachings.

— ॐ —

कायेन मनसा बुद्ध्या केवलैरिन्द्रियैरपि ।
kāyena manasā buddhyā kevalairindriyairapi
योगिनः कर्म कुर्वन्ति सङ्गं त्यक्त्वात्मशुद्धये ॥५-११॥
yoginaḥ karma kurvanti saṅgaṁ tyaktvātmaśuddhaye (5-11)

— ॐ —

कायेन मनसा बुद्ध्या केवलैरिन्द्रियैरपि ।
kāyena manasā buddhyā kevalairindriyairapi
योगिनः कर्म कुर्वन्ति सङ्गं त्यक्त्वात्मशुद्धये ॥५-११॥
yoginaḥ karma kurvanti saṅgaṁ tyaktvātmaśuddhaye (5-11)

ॐ तत्सदिति श्रीमद्भगवद्गीतासूपनिषत्सु ब्रह्मविद्यायां योगशास्त्रे श्रीकृष्णार्जुनसंवादे
om tatsaditi śrīmadbhagavadgītāsūpaniṣatsu brahmavidyāyāṁ yogaśāstre śrīkṛṣṇārjunasaṁvāde
संन्यासयोगो नाम पञ्चमोऽध्यायः श्लोकः ११
saṁnyāsayogo nāma pañcamo'dhyāyaḥ ślokaḥ 11

Om-Tat-Sat—Om (Braham) is the sole Reality. In the Yogic Scripture on the Science-of-Braham, the Shrimada-Bhāgvada-Gītā Upanishad, we hereby conclude Shloka 11 of the Dialogue between Shrī Krishna and Arjuna entitled Sanyāsa-Yoga, Canto V.

ॐ गीता श्लोकः ५.१२ – Gītā Verse 5.12

ॐ श्रीमद्भगवद्गीतासूपनिषत्सु ब्रह्मविद्यायां योगशास्त्रे श्रीकृष्णार्जुनसंवादे
om śrīmadbhagavadgītāsūpaniṣatsu brahmavidyāyāṁ yogaśāstre śrīkṛṣṇārjunasaṁvāde
संन्यासयोगो नाम पञ्चमोऽध्यायः श्लोकः १२
saṁnyāsayogo nāma pañcamo'dhyāyaḥ ślokaḥ 12

— ॐ —

युक्तः कर्मफलं त्यक्त्वा शान्तिमाप्नोति नैष्ठिकीम् ।
yuktaḥ karmaphalaṁ tyaktvā śāntimāpnoti naiṣṭhikīm
अयुक्तः कामकारेण फले सक्तो निबध्यते ॥५-१२॥
ayuktaḥ kāmakāreṇa phale sakto nibadhyate (5-12)

That harmonious one—integral in Yoga, giving up fruits of action—attains everlasting peace; whereas the unharmonious person—working under the sway of desires, hankering after fruits—gets ensnared. (5.12)

—: Word-by-Word :—

युक्तः yuktaḥ – the one who is united (in yoga); कर्मफलं karmaphalam – the fruit of action; त्यक्त्वा tyaktvā – having renounced; शान्तिम् śāntim – peace; आप्नोति āpnoti – attains; नैष्ठिकीम् naiṣṭhikīm – lasting; अयुक्तः ayuktaḥ – the unsteady one; कामकारेण kāmakāreṇa – impelled by desire; फले phale – in the result; सक्तः saktaḥ – attached; निबध्यते nibadhyate – becomes bound.

—: Understanding The Verse :—

— ॐ श्रीकृष्णाय नमः ॐ —

In this verse, Bhagwāna Shri Krishna reveals the divergent inner states and ultimate destinies of two types of individuals—the one who is steadfast in Yoga and the one who remains entangled in desire.

The former, established in equanimity and inner harmony युक्तः (Yuktaḥ), relinquishes all attachment to the fruits of action. Such a one does not act for gain, for reward, or even for spiritual pride. By this abandonment, he attains शान्तिम् नैष्ठिकीम् śāntim naiṣṭhikīm —a peace that is abiding and unshaken, born of self-integration and divine alignment.

In contrast stands the ayuktaḥ, the unintegrated man, driven by काम kāma (desire) and संग saṅga (attachment to outcome). Such a person, laboring for the fruits of action, is inevitably ensnared in the web of karma. His actions, far from liberating him, become chains that bind him to the cycle of birth and death.

This verse, then, serves as both an instruction and a warning. It extols the serenity of the renunciate-in-action and cautions against the inner unrest born of self-seeking deeds.

—: Key Sanskrit Terms :—

Let us uncover the latent wisdom of this verse through a close reading of its essential Sanskrit terms. We will discover how the renouncer of fruits finds peace, while the clinger to results stays bound and miserable. Each syllable here exhales freedom, unknots restlessness.

— ॐ —

युक्तः (Yuktaḥ):

The युक्तः yuktaḥ — the one harmonized in Yoga — refers to the soul who has yoked his mind, body, and intellect to the Divine through detachment and surrender.

His actions flow from stillness, and thus, they leave no residue.

— ॐ —

कर्मफलम् त्यक्त्वा (Karma-phalaṁ tyaktvā):

Renouncing the कर्मफलम् karma-phalam — the fruits of action — is not a refusal to act, but a refusal to be bound by the results.

Action is performed as an offering, its outcome left in the hands of the Supreme.

The giving up of fruits is the giving up of anxiety, pride, and regret.

— ॐ —

शान्तिम् आप्नोति नैष्ठिकीम् (Śāntim āpnoti naiṣṭhikīm):

शान्ति Śānti — peace — is not merely emotional calm but the profound stillness of realization.

नैष्ठिकी शान्ति Naiṣṭhikī śānti is the peace that is unshakable, rooted in the certitude of the Self — eternal, immutable, and free.

— ॐ —

अयुक्तः (Ayuktaḥ):

The अयुक्तः ayuktaḥ — the unharmonized being — is one whose heart is scattered by desires, whose actions are tainted by craving, whose mind is tethered to the wheel of gain and loss.

— ॐ —

कामकारेण फले सक्तः निबध्यते (Kāmakāreṇa phale saktaḥ nibadhyate):

Compelled by काम kāma (desire), the अयुक्तः ayuktaḥ clings to the fruits of actions, and thus is निबध्यते nibadhyate — bound, fettered ever tighter into the endless cycles of birth and death.

His action, rather than liberating, thickens the veils of ignorance.

The phrases in this verse unfold the two destinies: the serene flowering of the liberated soul, and the restless entanglement of the unawakened.

—: In Brief :—

— ॐ श्रीकृष्णाय नमः ॐ —

In this verse, Shri Krishna distinguishes between the युक्तः Yuktaḥ—the one united with Yoga—and the अयुक्तः Ayuktaḥ—the one estranged from it.

The अयुक्तः Yuktaḥ, having renounced the fruits of all action, attains peace—not a mere emotional stillness, but the deep and enduring tranquility of the self शाश्वत शान्ति (śāśvat śānti), untouched by dualities and anchored in the Divine.

The word युक्तः Yuktaḥ, derived from the root 'yuj', meaning "to join" or "to yoke," has various contextual shades across the Gītā. In some verses, it denotes a person of steady wisdom; in others, one of ascetic control or equanimous discipline. Here, the term clearly refers to a कर्म-योगी Karma-Yogi—a practitioner of action who is inwardly free.

The Karma-Yogi does not cease to act; rather, he relinquishes the self-interest normally tethered to action. His work is not a means of self-aggrandizement, but a quiet expression of devotion and inner alignment. Thus, such a person abides in peace.

— ॐ श्रीरामाय नमः ॐ —

On the other hand, the अयुक्तः Ayuktaḥ is not merely one who lacks physical discipline or knowledge, but one who is fundamentally driven by desire.

He clings to the fruits of his endeavors, working not in a spirit of offering, but of grasping. As a result, his karma binds him. The very actions that should have uplifted him instead become a cause of bondage निबध्यते (nibadhyate), for desire infects the will, and attachment entangles the soul.

The contrast is thus not in action itself, but in the motive and attitude with which action is undertaken.

The युक्तः Yuktaḥ moves in the world as a servant of Dharma, a silent pilgrim on the inner path; the अयुक्तः Ayuktaḥ remains tossed in the storm of expectation and the tyranny of outcomes.

— ॐ विश्वामित्रप्रियाय नमः ॐ —

This verse is not just a comparison—it is a forked path, and every seeker must choose. Shall one act in bondage, or act in freedom? Shall one be driven by the ego's hunger, or shall one act as a consecrated instrument of the Divine?

Having shown the superiority of renunciation of fruits, Bhagwāna Shri Krishna now turns, in the subsequent verses, to further unveil the state of the ज्ञानी Jñānī—the one who sees all beings with equal vision, who has transcended not only attachment but also the very distinction between self and other. Thus, the teaching deepens from action to wisdom, from discipline to realization.

— ॐ तत सत ॐ —

Before we move on, let us bow in reverence to this sacred verse. Write it by hand, reflect on its meaning, chant it aloud, make it your own.

— ॐ —

युक्तः कर्मफलं त्यक्त्वा शान्तिमाप्नोति नैष्ठिकीम् ।
yuktaḥ karmaphalaṁ tyaktvā śāntimāpnoti naiṣṭhikīm
अयुक्तः कामकारेण फले सक्तो निबध्यते ॥५-१२॥
ayuktaḥ kāmakāreṇa phale sakto nibadhyate (5-12)

युक्तः कर्मफलं त्यक्त्वा शान्तिमाप्नोति नैष्ठिकीम् ।
yuktaḥ karmaphalaṁ tyaktvā śāntimāpnoti naiṣṭhikīm
अयुक्तः कामकारेण फले सक्तो निबध्यते ॥५-१२॥
ayuktaḥ kāmakāreṇa phale sakto nibadhyate (5-12)

ॐ तत्सदिति श्रीमद्भगवद्गीतासूपनिषत्सु ब्रह्मविद्यायां योगशास्त्रे श्रीकृष्णार्जुनसंवादे
om tatsaditi śrīmadbhagavadgītāsūpaniṣatsu brahmavidyāyāṁ yogaśāstre śrīkṛṣṇārjunasaṁvāde
संन्यासयोगो नाम पञ्चमोऽध्यायः श्लोकः १२
saṁnyāsayogo nāma pañcamo'dhyāyaḥ ślokaḥ 12

Om-Tat-Sat—Om (Braham) is the sole Reality. In the Yogic Scripture on the Science-of-Braham, the Shrimada-Bhāgvada-Gītā Upanishad, we hereby conclude Shloka 12 of the Dialogue between Shrī Krishna and Arjuna entitled Sanyāsa-Yoga, Canto V.

We see the field being carved by a plough,
But who really knows what impels man? What has hewed his soul?

<u>Behold, Two Men are Seen Working,</u>
They look the same, but are so different—
For who really can view a man's mind to figure out the difference?
One walks free. The other coils in shadows.
One gives our fruit and corn—the other makes and eats thorns.
Peace, says the Lord, is not necessarily in silence—
It is in surrender.
The Yogi acts—and yields the fruit.
The other acts to devour everything—before then devouring himself.

ॐ गीता श्लोकः ५.१३ – GĪTĀ VERSE 5.13

ॐ श्रीमद्भगवद्गीतासूपनिषत्सु ब्रह्मविद्यायां योगशास्त्रे श्रीकृष्णार्जुनसंवादे
om śrīmadbhagavadgītāsūpaniṣatsu brahmavidyāyāṁ yogaśāstre śrīkṛṣṇārjunasaṁvāde
संन्यासयोगो नाम पञ्चमोऽध्यायः श्लोकः १३
saṁnyāsayogo nāma pañcamo'dhyāyaḥ ślokaḥ 13

— ॐ —

सर्वकर्माणि मनसा संन्यस्यास्ते सुखं वशी ।
sarvakarmāṇi manasā saṁnyasyāste sukhaṁ vaśī
नवद्वारे पुरे देही नैव कुर्वन्न कारयन् ॥५-१३॥
navadvāre pure dehī naiva kurvanna kārayan (5-13)

The self-controlled one, mentally renouncing all actions, rests at ease and in peace—like an embodied soul, living merely as an indweller abiding within the city of nine-gates (the body)—neither acting nor causing to act. (5.13)

—: Word-by-Word :—

सर्वकर्माणि sarvakarmāṇi – all actions; मनसा manasā – with the mind; संन्यस्य saṁnyasya – renouncing; आस्ते āste – rests; सुखम् sukham – in happiness; वशी vaśī – self-controlled; नवद्वारे navadvāre – in the city of nine gates; पुरे pure – in the body; देही dehī – the embodied soul; न na – neither; एव eva – indeed; कुर्वन् kurvan – acting; न na – nor; कारयन् kārayan – causing (others to act).

—: Understanding The Verse :—

— ॐ श्रीकृष्णाय नमः ॐ —

In this verse, Bhagwāna Shri Krishna unveils the inward posture of the one who has truly renounced action—not through external abandonment, but by an inner act of discernment. He describes the Sankhya-Yogi, the discriminating sage, who, though still embodied, abides in deep repose, unaffected by the play of action and inaction.

Such a one, having mentally relinquished all actions, dwells at peace within the body, which is poetically referred to as the city of nine gates—symbolizing the body's sense apertures and operative faculties.

Yet, though residing in the body, this sage neither acts nor impels others to act. His apparent engagement with the world is superficial, like a lotus leaf on water—touched, yet untouched.

— ॐ श्रीरामाय नमः ॐ —

This verse underscores the inward renunciation of doership कर्तव्य अभिमान त्याग (kartṛtva-abhimāna-tyāga) as the heart of true spiritual repose.

It further clarifies that renunciation does not mean physical withdrawal or passivity, but the complete dissolution of ego-identification with action.

—: Key Sanskrit Terms :—

Let us approach the heart of this verse by reflecting on the significant Sanskrit words that weave its deeper insights. Each word here is alike a hermit closing the gate of his hut. Dwelling in the city of nine gates, unattached, he neither acts nor causes action. Each word holds the verse firm—then withdraws softly inward, into stillness.

— ॐ —

सर्वकर्माणि मनसा संन्यस्य (Sarvakarmāṇi manasā saṁnyasya):
By "mentally renouncing all actions," the seeker (yogin) does not cease outer activities but internally abandons ownership and desire.
संन्यास Saṁnyāsa here signifies an inner offering, wherein all deeds are relinquished into the fire of Self-knowledge.
True renunciation is a withdrawal of identification, not a negation of life's flow.

— ॐ —

आस्ते सुखं वशी (Āste sukhaṁ vaśī):
The वशी vaśī — the self-governed one, master of body and senses — abides आस्ते (āste) in सुख sukha — not mere worldly happiness, but the deep, luminous ease of the soul that has become its own sovereign.
He lives in the world as a lotus lives upon water: untouched, serene, fulfilled.

— ॐ —

नवद्वारे पुरे देही (Navadvāre pure dehī):
The body is likened to a पुर pura — a city — with nine gates नवद्वार (nava-dvāra): the eyes, ears, nostrils, mouth, excretory, and reproductive openings.
The देही dehī, the embodied soul, dwells within, observing the city's functions, but no longer entangled by its bustle.
The metaphor conveys profound detachment — witnessing without entrapment.

— ॐ —

नैव कुर्वन् न कारयन् (Naiva kurvan na kārayan):

Neither acting नैव कुर्वन् (naiva kurvan) nor causing others to act न कारयन् (na kārayan): the Self remains the silent witness, neither engaging directly nor indirectly in the operations of प्रकृति prakṛti.

Action belongs to nature; being belongs to the Self.

Every terms here which Bhagwāna Shri Krishna speaks, delicately portrays the life of the liberated one — moving amidst the world's myriad activities while inwardly abiding in a changeless stillness.

—: In Brief :—

— ॐ श्रीकृष्णाय नमः ॐ —

Here, Shri Krishna continues to illuminate the subtle truth of inner renunciation, presenting the image of the self-controlled sage who, having withdrawn the sense of agency through discernment, rests in serene detachment.

The phrase "मनसा सर्वाणि कर्माणि संन्यस्यास् manasā sarvāṇi karmāṇi sannyasya"—having mentally renounced all actions—does not denote a cessation of activity at the physical level, but a profound disengagement from the false notion, "I am the doer."

— ॐ वनवासप्रियाय नमः ॐ —

The sage, though living in the body—described here as the nine-gated city नवद्वारे पुरे (nava-dvāre pure)—neither acts nor causes others to act.

The metaphor of the city with nine gates refers to the nine openings of the human body—two eyes, two ears, two nostrils, mouth, and the two lower apertures—through which the senses operate and life expresses itself.

This metaphor is not incidental; it implies that the body, like a city, is merely a vehicle of operations. The true Self, the देही dehī, is the indwelling witness, residing therein—who abides aloof, and never becomes entangled in the word.

— ॐ सौम्याय नमः ॐ —

With this vision, Bhagwāna Shri Krishna leads us closer to the realization of Braham, by preparing the seeker to discern the Self from the not-Self.

The verses which follow further deepen this insight, showing how all actions arise from Prakṛti, and the Self remains ever-actionless—ever-free.

— ॐ तत सत ॐ —

Before moving on, let us once more bow in deep reverence before this sacred verse of the Bhagavad-Gītā, an eternal beacon of wisdom that ceaselessly illumines the path of seekers. Engage with its form—inscribe it with your own hand, let your heart dwell upon its meaning, and raise your voice in its chanting—for within these syllables echoes the undying proclamation delivered millennia ago on the battlefield of Kurukshetra. These words, transmitted unchanged across the unbroken chain of generations, form a living bridge, linking us to that sanctified era when Bhagwāna Shri Krishna Himself walked this earth and bestowed this divine teaching. Through the luminous vibration of these sacred Sanskrit sounds, we are drawn nearer to His timeless presence, touching the very heartbeat of the Eternal.

— ॐ —

सर्वकर्माणि मनसा संन्यस्यास्ते सुखं वशी ।
sarvakarmāṇi manasā saṁnyasyāste sukhaṁ vaśī
नवद्वारे पुरे देही नैव कुर्वन्न कारयन् ॥५-१३॥
navadvāre pure dehī naiva kurvanna kārayan (5-13)

— ॐ —
सर्वकर्माणि मनसा संन्यस्यास्ते सुखं वशी ।
sarvakarmāṇi manasā saṁnyasyāste sukhaṁ vaśī
नवद्वारे पुरे देही नैव कुर्वन्न कारयन् ॥५-१३॥
navadvāre pure dehī naiva kurvanna kārayan (5-13)

ॐ तत्सदिति श्रीमद्भगवद्गीतासूपनिषत्सु ब्रह्मविद्यायां योगशास्त्रे श्रीकृष्णार्जुनसंवादे
om tatsaditi śrīmadbhagavadgītāsūpaniṣatsu brahmavidyāyāṁ yogaśāstre śrīkṛṣṇārjunasaṁvāde
संन्यासयोगो नाम पञ्चमोऽध्यायः श्लोकः १३
saṁnyāsayogo nāma pañcamo'dhyāyaḥ ślokaḥ 13

Om-Tat-Sat—Om (Braham) is the sole Reality. In the Yogic Scripture on the Science-of-Braham, the Shrimada-Bhāgvada-Gītā Upanishad, we hereby conclude Shloka 13 of the Dialogue between Shrī Krishna and Arjuna entitled Sanyāsa-Yoga, Canto V.

— ॐ सौमित्रिप्रियसखाय नमः ॐ —

The Karma-Yogi acts with hands,
with thoughts, with words—
but he owns no motion.
He serves Sanātana-Dharma.
But he does not serve to gain anything.
He serves to burn the fog—
Which may still cling to the mirror of the Self.

ॐ गीता श्लोकः ५.१४ – GĪTĀ VERSE 5.14

ॐ श्रीमद्भगवद्गीतासूपनिषत्सु ब्रह्मविद्यायां योगशास्त्रे श्रीकृष्णार्जुनसंवादे
om śrīmadbhagavadgītāsūpaniṣatsu brahmavidyāyāṁ yogaśāstre śrīkṛṣṇārjunasaṁvāde
संन्यासयोगो नाम पञ्चमोऽध्यायः श्लोकः १४
saṁnyāsayogo nāma pañcamo'dhyāyaḥ ślokaḥ 14

— ॐ —

न कर्तृत्वं न कर्माणि लोकस्य सृजति प्रभुः ।
na kartṛtvaṁ na karmāṇi lokasya sṛjati prabhuḥ
न कर्मफलसंयोगं स्वभावस्तु प्रवर्तते ॥५-१४॥
na karmaphalasaṁyogaṁ svabhāvastu pravartate (5-14)

God creates for this world neither the doership, nor the doings, nor either the union with the fruits of doings—it is only Nature which enacts, reacts and performs in its natural course. (5.14)

—: Word-by-Word :—

न na – neither; कर्तृत्वम् kartṛtvam – agency; न na – nor; कर्माणि karmāṇi – actions; लोकस्य lokasya – of the world; सृजति sṛjati – does create; प्रभुः prabhuḥ – the Lord; न na – nor; कर्मफलसंयोगम् karmaphala-saṁyogam – connection with the fruits of actions; स्वभावः svabhāvaḥ – nature; तु tu – rather; प्रवर्तते pravartate – acts.

—: Understanding The Verse :—

— ॐ श्रीकृष्णाय नमः ॐ —

In this verse, Bhagwāna Shri Krishna lifts the veil on a subtle metaphysical truth concerning the nature of agency and action.

Addressing the error that binds the soul to the cycle of karma, the Lord declares: the Supreme—though the creator, sustainer, and dissolver of the cosmos—does not assign doership to individuals, nor does He ordain actions or their linkage with fruits.

Instead, it is प्रकृति Prakṛti, Nature endowed with the three guṇas—sattva, rajas, and tamas—which carries out all functions. The Self, being of the nature of सत-चित-आनन्द sat-cit-ānanda (existence-consciousness-bliss), remains ever-untouched, ever-pure, ever-free.

Thus, this verse serves as a corrective to the misapprehension that God is the direct architect of every individual action or moral destiny. It underscores the distinction between the immutable Self and the mutable play of Nature, reminding the seeker to shift his identification from the latter to the former.

—: Key Sanskrit Terms :—

Let us pause to consider the verse's principal expressions. By concentrating on the verse's core Sanskrit vocabulary, we can unlock hidden shades of meaning that will enrich our understanding. Each word here is line an actor for hire—who has had endless roles in literature, in different verses, in varied circumstance. In this verse of the Gitā, each word portrays an elightened Yogi who has stepped off the worldly stage. The Self neither creates action, nor agency, nor union of results; nature alone unfolds them. Each syllable strips illusion from the script.

— ॐ —

न कर्तृत्वं न कर्माणि (Na kartṛtvaṁ na karmāṇi):

कर्तृत्वं Kartṛtva — the sense of "I am the doer" — and कर्माणि karmāṇi — the actions themselves — are both negated as not originating from the Supreme प्रभुः (prabhuḥ).

The Lord does not create the bondage of agency or deeds; they belong to another realm — the realm of ignorance and प्रकृति prakṛti.

— ॐ —

लोकस्य सृजति प्रभुः (Lokasya sṛjati prabhuḥ):

The प्रभुः prabhuḥ — the Supreme Lord, the transcendent Master — does not entangle the souls in the meshes of action and reaction.

The प्रभु Divine remains the pure Witness, the silent foundation of all.

— ॐ —

न कर्मफलसंयोगम् (Na karmaphalasaṁyogam):

Nor does God arrange the संयोगम् union of कर्म action with its फल fruit.

The binding together of deed and consequence is a mechanical law within प्रकृति prakṛti, not a decree imposed by the Self-luminous Reality.

— ॐ —

स्वभावः तु प्रवर्तते (Svabhāvaḥ tu pravartate):

स्वभावः Svabhāva — the innate nature, the inborn tendency of प्रकृति prakṛti — alone is the agent.

Nature, with its गुण guṇas (sattva, rajas, tamas), acts according to its own inherent laws.

Souls become entangled not by divine imposition, but by identification with this restless स्वभाव svabhāva.

Each terms delicately distinguishes the immutable Spirit from the mutable activities of Nature, clarifying the source of bondage and the path to freedom.

—: In Brief :—

— ॐ श्रीकृष्णाय नमः ॐ —

In this verse, Bhagwāna Shri Krishna dispels a foundational delusion that underlies human bondage—the false attribution of doership to the Self, and of divine ordination to individual action.

The word प्रभुः Prabhuḥ here refers not to the impersonal Self (Ātmā), but to ईश्वर Īśvara, the Lord as Creator and Sustainer.

Even so, Krishna asserts that God does not ordain the कर्तृत्वम् kartṛtvam (doership), कर्माणि karmāṇi (actions), or कर्म-फल-संयोग karma-phala-saṅyoga (connection with the fruits of action) for the beings in this world.

These do not proceed from God's decree, but arise from प्रकृति Prakṛti—from the cosmic energy governed by the modes of Nature, or Gunas.

— ॐ श्रीरामाय नमः ॐ —

Why is this clarification essential?

Because if God were directly assigning good or evil deeds, and the results thereof, then the entire framework of Dharma, अधिकार adhikāra (individual responsibility), and साधना sādhana (spiritual striving) would collapse.

The scriptures' injunctions and prohibitions would lose their meaning. Human freedom would be a spoof, and deliverance would be impossible. The लीला Lila of Krishna would itself become a mockery, if everything was preordained, or God was involved in the nitty-gritty of things.

No O motral: He just created the laws, and wound up the spring, and then He set the balls rolling—to enjoy the show.

Let us never un-remember : This whole show is a sport of Braham.

— ॐ खरदूषणसंहारिणे नमः ॐ —

Here Krishna reveals a deeper order: the soul, in truth, is neither the doer nor the enjoyer.

Action belongs to प्रकृति Prakṛti, which operates through the senses, mind, and intellect—through the conditioning of the guṇas.

The ignorant, deluded by अहंकार ahaṅkāra (egoism), mistake themselves as the doer. This very ignorance is the bondage.

But the one who sees that all activity is but the unfolding of Prakṛti, and that the Self is a witness alone—such a one becomes free.

See how this verse harmonizes with the earlier teaching of 3.27:

प्रकृतेः क्रियमाणानि गुणैः कर्माणि सर्वशः । अहङ्कारविमूढात्मा कर्ताहमिति मन्यते ॥३-२७॥
prakṛteḥ kriyamāṇāni guṇaiḥ karmāṇi sarvaśaḥ,
ahaṅkāravimūḍhātmā kartāhamiti manyate.

[It is Nature that performs all actions, but the deluded self, blinded by ego, claims, "I am the doer." Verse 3.27]

— ॐ श्रीनारायणाय नमः ॐ —

In asserting that God does not connect the soul with the fruits of action, Krishna points to a crucial truth: it is attachment and ignorance that forge the link between karma and bondage.

When these are dissolved, the soul, though still appearing to act, remains untouched, like the sun illumining all yet bound to none.

This verse continues the Bhagavad-Gītā's majestic dismantling of spiritual ignorance.

It reaffirms the freedom of the Self, clarifies the autonomous operation of Prakṛti, and prepares us seekers for the sublime teaching that follows: if neither the Self nor God is entangled in action, then how are beings to attain the fruit of their actions?

The next verse answers this, deepening our understanding of delusion मोह (moha) and liberation मोक्ष (mokṣa).

— ॐ तत सत ॐ —

Before moving on, let us once more bow in deep reverence before this sacred verse of the Bhagavad-Gītā, an eternal beacon of wisdom that ceaselessly illumines the path of seekers. Engage with its form—inscribe it with your own hand, let your heart dwell upon its meaning, and raise your voice in its chanting—for within these syllables echoes the undying proclamation delivered millennia ago on the battlefield of Kurukshetra. These words, transmitted unchanged across the unbroken chain of generations, form a living bridge, linking us to that sanctified era when Bhagwāna Shri Krishna Himself walked this earth and bestowed this divine teaching. Through the luminous vibration of these sacred Sanskrit sounds, we are drawn nearer to His timeless presence, touching the very heartbeat of the Eternal.

— ॐ —

न कर्तृत्वं न कर्माणि लोकस्य सृजति प्रभुः ।
na kartṛtvaṁ na karmāṇi lokasya sṛjati prabhuḥ
न कर्मफलसंयोगं स्वभावस्तु प्रवर्तते ॥५-१४॥
na karmaphalasaṁyogaṁ svabhāvastu pravartate (5-14)

— ॐ —

न कर्तृत्वं न कर्माणि लोकस्य सृजति प्रभुः ।
na kartṛtvaṁ na karmāṇi lokasya sṛjati prabhuḥ
न कर्मफलसंयोगं स्वभावस्तु प्रवर्तते ॥५-१४॥
na karmaphalasaṁyogaṁ svabhāvastu pravartate (5-14)

ॐ तत्सदिति श्रीमद्भगवद्गीतासूपनिषत्सु ब्रह्मविद्यायां योगशास्त्रे श्रीकृष्णार्जुनसंवादे
om tatsaditi śrīmadbhagavadgītāsūpaniṣatsu brahmavidyāyāṁ yogaśāstre śrīkṛṣṇārjunasaṁvāde
संन्यासयोगो नाम पञ्चमोऽध्यायः श्लोकः १४
saṁnyāsayogo nāma pañcamo'dhyāyaḥ ślokaḥ 14

Om-Tat-Sat—Om (Braham) is the sole Reality. In the Yogic Scripture on the Science-of-Braham, the Shrimada-Bhāgvada-Gītā Upanishad, we hereby conclude Shloka 14 of the Dialogue between Shrī Krishna and Arjuna entitled Sanyāsa-Yoga, Canto V.

— ॐ धर्मरक्षकाय नमः ॐ —

A Clean Blade Through the Illusion of 'Cause'.

Braham weaves no threads of blame and praise.
No punishment He doles. Nor reward for any favorites of His.
No ostensible favored-son sitting to His right.
No exclusive messenger-prophet s.o.b—
with angels whispering secrets into greasy dirty hairy ears.

– o –

God follows no bookmarked directions—
Has not even a preferred species.
Has no volitions that serve any aim.
No targets to reach. No goals.
Beyond the fun of ingenious creativity, God does not do anything at all!
All Doership in Him is imagined by foolish humans.

– o –

Braham created Prakriti—Nature with its cosmic laws,
then set the balls rolling—to interact, react, play.
The endless deeds happening in the cosmos –

are just ripples in the ocean-of-consciousness of His.
Nature intersects, collides, reacts, strikes back—
Aloof, unconcerned, God simply watches—the Show playing out.

– o –

Zillions of years later enters a lil homo-sapien on a lil earth—
A darting flash flew off God's endlessly revolving giant wheel—
A passing spark, here now gone the next—a blip if you will.
But the intoxicated groggy man assigns for himself a topmost place,

– o –

Man calls himself the very darling of God—
privileged to rule over all that fly, swim, crawl.
He ascribes a Ruler's role for himself on the globe—
and assigns a purpose to God's alleged 'Plan', in which:
Arrogating all things and creatures of earth for himself—
And dominion over other men too—if they refuse to follow
'my god', 'my savior', 'my-book'—
he then gets god's license to kill and ravage,
And he would then kill, rape, loot, plunder, break idols,
and call it 'religion'
—which two malignant 'religious' sects have by now devoured
Over half the world like cancer.

– o –

Blind to the gunas at play, man hollers and claims:
"This is me—my brain, my hand, my deed, my craft, my very handiwork;
O look at me, see how smart I am!"
Drunk on delusion the puppet now calls himself the master.
When the going is good, man claims all thunder,
Oft, most would keep sucking up to God praying for this or that payoff.
When things go wrong they curse the sky and blame the God.

– o –

Alas, all that the pestiferous human has ended up doing is:
Destruct the earth and butcher Braham's sport, His play.
Plus this foolish animal has built his very own cage of bondages—
wherein he lives nestled life after life.
But not for long though—for God's justice cometh.
For none botches His Leela, destroys Sanātana-Dharma—
and not get smacked back hard.

ॐ गीता श्लोकः ५.१५ – GĪTĀ VERSE 5.15

ॐ श्रीमद्भगवद्गीतासूपनिषत्सु ब्रह्मविद्यायां योगशास्त्रे श्रीकृष्णार्जुनसंवादे
om śrīmadbhagavadgītāsūpaniṣatsu brahmavidyāyāṁ yogaśāstre śrīkṛṣṇārjunasaṁvāde
संन्यासयोगो नाम पञ्चमोऽध्यायः श्लोकः १५
saṁnyāsayogo nāma pañcamo'dhyāyaḥ ślokaḥ 15

— ॐ —

नादत्ते कस्यचित्पापं न चैव सुकृतं विभुः ।
nādatte kasyacitpāpaṁ na caiva sukṛtaṁ vibhuḥ
अज्ञानेनावृतं ज्ञानं तेन मुह्यन्ति जन्तवः ॥५-१५॥
ajñānenāvṛtaṁ jñānaṁ tena muhyanti jantavaḥ (5-15)

The Lord-God—present everywhere and the same to all—is never really involved with the sins or virtues of any beings. But because Truth remains clouded in Ignorance, the embodied beings of the world persist bewildered.
(5.15)

—: *Word-by-Word* :—

न आदत्ते na ādatte – does not accept; कस्यचित् kasyacit – anyone's; पापम् pāpam – sin; न na – nor; च एव ca eva – indeed; सुकृतम् sukṛtam – virtue; विभुः vibhuḥ – the all-pervading Lord; अज्ञानेन ajñānena – by ignorance; आवृतम् āvṛtam – covered; ज्ञानम् jñānam – knowledge; तेन tena – by that; मुह्यन्ति muhyanti – are deluded; जन्तवः jantavaḥ – beings.

—: *Understanding The Verse* :—

— ॐ श्रीकृष्णाय नमः ॐ —

In this verse, Bhagwāna Shri Krishna dispels yet another subtle misconception that clouds the seeker's understanding: the idea that the Lord, or the Self, partakes in the moral residue—पुण्य पाप puṇya and pāpa—of the actions performed by beings.

Shri Krishna declares that the Lord neither accepts virtue nor vice from anyone. The pure Self, being untainted, omnipresent, and unchanging, remains ever detached from the dualities of good and evil. The reason beings are bewildered lies not in divine injustice or interference, but in their own ignorance—which veils true knowledge and fosters delusion.

Thus, this verse underscores the non-doership and impartiality of the Self. It is not the Supreme who binds the soul, but अविद्या Avidyā—the darkness of ignorance—that entangles beings in confusion, delusion, and repeated birth.

—: Key Sanskrit Terms :—

To grasp the subtle teachings embedded in this śloka, let us first attend to the layered meanings of its Sanskrit words—each word shining like light dissipating shadows away.

The light may reveal good or ugly, but the lamp itself stays unsullied by both; similarly, the words themselves stay untarnished, whatever meaning we may construe out of them. And so too the Lord-God takes neither sin nor merit of anyone—even as the sky stays unsoiled by smoke.

— ॐ —

न आदत्ते कस्यचित् पापं (Na ādatte kasyacit pāpam):

The Supreme Lord, the Self of all, does not आदत्ते ādatté — "take" or "accept" — the sins of any being.

Sin पाप (pāpa) is not attributed by God as reward or punishment; it is self-woven by the being through identification with ignorance and action.

— ॐ —

न च एव सुकृतं (Na ca eva sukṛtam):

Nor does the Lord seize or own the merits सुकृतं (sukṛtam).

The divine Reality remains ever the impartial Witness, untouched by the dualities of good and evil, virtue and vice, which belong to the realm of प्रकृति prakṛti and the embodied soul.

— ॐ —

विभुः (Vibhuḥ):

विभुः Vibhuḥ — "the All-pervading" — signifies the Supreme Being who is infinite, omnipresent, transcendent, and immanent.

Vast and free, the Lord dwells within all, but is stained by none, much as the sun remains unsullied by the impurities of the earth it illumines.

— ॐ —

अज्ञानेनावृतं ज्ञानं (Ajñānenāvṛtaṁ jñānam):

Here, the profound mechanism of bondage is revealed:

ज्ञान jñāna — the innate light of the Self — is veiled आवृतं (āvṛtam) by अज्ञान ajñāna — ignorance.

This veiling does not destroy knowledge, but conceals it, like clouds covering the radiant sun.

— ॐ —

तेन मुह्यन्ति जन्तवः (Tena muhyanti jantavaḥ):

Because of this covering, जन्तवः jantavaḥ — living beings — fall into moha, bewilderment and delusion. Identifying with body, mind, and senses, they lose sight of their own divine essence and wander in the darkness of संसार saṁsāra.

Every phrase above delicately illuminates the untouched purity of the Divine and the self-created delusion of the embodied soul.

—: In Brief :—

— ॐ श्रीकृष्णाय नमः ॐ —

Bhagwāna Shri Krishna here affirms a core truth of Vedānta: the Supreme Self—विभुः Vibhuḥ, the all-pervading, unconditioned Reality—does not appropriate to Itself the moral burden of human actions.

नादत्ते कस्यचित्पापं न चैव सुकृतं Na adatte kasyacit pāpam na ca eva sukṛtam—the Lord does not accept either sin or virtue from any being.

This detachment does not stem just from supreme aloofness, but from divine completeness. The Self is ever-full पूर्ण (pūrṇa), beyond desire, untouched by the fruits of karma.

— ॐ सर्वपापहराय नमः ॐ —

Though beings act, and reap results in the form of joy and suffering, it is not the Lord who orchestrates these in a partial or prejudiced manner.

The root of their bondage lies in अज्ञान ajñāna—ignorance. अज्ञानेनावृतं ज्ञानं ajñānenāvṛtaṁ jñānaṁ —knowledge is veiled by ignorance.

And it is this veiling that gives rise to मोह moha—delusion, which causes beings to identify themselves with the body, the mind, and the ego, and thus to become entangled in doership and enjoyership.

— ॐ श्रीकेशवाय नमः ॐ —

So then what causes bondage?

Yes, it is मोह जाल moha-jāla—the net of delusion spun by अज्ञान ajñāna.

When this ignorance is dispelled by ज्ञान jñāna—true knowledge—then the being sees that the Self was never bound, never touched, never changed.

This sets the stage for the next verse, where Shri Krishna begins to describe the awakened ones, those in whom ignorance has been destroyed, and whose vision rests firmly established in Truth.

— ॐ तत सत ॐ —

Before we move on, let us bow in reverence to this sacred verse. Write it by hand, reflect on its meaning, chant it aloud, make it your own.

— ॐ —

नादत्ते कस्यचित्पापं न चैव सुकृतं विभुः ।
nādatte kasyacitpāpaṁ na caiva sukṛtaṁ vibhuḥ
अज्ञानेनावृतं ज्ञानं तेन मुह्यन्ति जन्तवः ॥५-१५॥
ajñānenāvṛtaṁ jñānaṁ tena muhyanti jantavaḥ (5-15)

— ॐ —

नादत्ते कस्यचित्पापं न चैव सुकृतं विभुः ।
nādatte kasyacitpāpaṁ na caiva sukṛtaṁ vibhuḥ
अज्ञानेनावृतं ज्ञानं तेन मुह्यन्ति जन्तवः ॥५-१५॥
ajñānenāvṛtaṁ jñānaṁ tena muhyanti jantavaḥ (5-15)

ॐ तत्सदिति श्रीमद्भगवद्गीतासूपनिषत्सु ब्रह्मविद्यायां योगशास्त्रे श्रीकृष्णार्जुनसंवादे
om tatsaditi śrīmadbhagavadgītāsūpaniṣatsu brahmavidyāyāṁ yogaśāstre śrīkṛṣṇārjunasaṁvāde
संन्यासयोगो नाम पञ्चमोऽध्यायः श्लोकः १५
saṁnyāsayogo nāma pañcamo'dhyāyaḥ ślokaḥ 15

Om-Tat-Sat—Om (Braham) is the sole Reality. In the Yogic Scripture on the Science-of-Braham, the Shrimada-Bhāgvada-Gītā Upanishad, we hereby conclude Shloka 15 of the Dialogue between Shrī Krishna and Arjuna entitled Sanyāsa-Yoga, Canto V.

— ॐ योगिनां पतये नमः ॐ —

O mind, thou weepest, "Fate is cruel,"
Yet bindest thyself more in thy own created bondages!
Thou criest, "Why this pain, this night?"—
But thou wear'st the very veil which has dimmed the Light.

The Lord, all-pure, accepts no stain—
Yet I heap more guilt, and I grieve again.
It is not He who judges, strikes, inveighs, or weighs—
'Tis I who strayed — into ugly shadowy ways.
O blinded soul, dost thou still not see—
Thy prison was forged, by none other than thee?

O me, arise from sorrow's snare—
The Lord accepts no guilt of thine, nor curse or glare.
He holds not vice nor virtue near—
He shines in peace, serene and clear.
It is not He who writes thy fate,
But it's thee—who has chosen to sleep even at Truth's gate!

O fool, cast off the cloak of "mine" and "me,"
And know thy Self to be completely free.
No Lord above thy sin has stored;
Alas—it's thee who has chosen Ignorance to be thy false lord—
While spurning Bhagwana Shri Krishna: the Real Lord-God!

ॐ गीता श्लोकः ५.१६ – Gītā Verse 5.16

ॐ श्रीमद्भगवद्गीतासूपनिषत्सु ब्रह्मविद्यायां योगशास्त्रे श्रीकृष्णार्जुनसंवादे
om śrīmadbhagavadgītāsūpaniṣatsu brahmavidyāyāṁ yogaśāstre śrīkṛṣṇārjunasaṁvāde
संन्यासयोगो नाम पञ्चमोऽध्यायः श्लोकः १६
saṁnyāsayogo nāma pañcamo'dhyāyaḥ ślokaḥ 16

— ॐ —

ज्ञानेन तु तदज्ञानं येषां नाशितमात्मनः ।
jñānena tu tadajñānaṁ yeṣāṁ nāśitamātmanaḥ
तेषामादित्यवज्ज्ञानं प्रकाशयति तत्परम् ॥५-१६॥
teṣāmādityavajjñānaṁ prakāśayati tatparam (5-16)

But when Nescience is destroyed in the light of the Knowledge of the Self, then the mind, shining like the sun, reveals everything—right up to that Supreme-Being. (5.16)

—: Word-by-Word :—

ज्ञानेन jñānena – by knowledge; तु tu – however; तत् tat – that; अज्ञानम् ajñānam – ignorance; येषाम् yeṣām – whose; नाशितम् nāśitam – is destroyed; आत्मनः ātmanaḥ – of the self; तेषाम् teṣām – for them; आदित्यवत् ādityavat – like the sun; ज्ञानम् jñānam – knowledge; प्रकाशयति prakāśayati – reveals; तत् tat – that; परम् param – the supreme.

—: Understanding The Verse :—

— ॐ श्रीकृष्णाय नमः ॐ —

In this luminous verse, Bhagwāna Shri Krishna proclaims the power of Self-knowledge आत्म -ज्ञान (Ātma-Jñāna) to dispel the darkness of ignorance अज्ञान (ajñāna), which veils the vision of Truth.

He affirms that when this fundamental delusion is destroyed, the inner light of wisdom dawns, illuminating all aspects of reality—even up to the Supreme Being परम-ब्रह्म (Parama-Braham).

— ॐ श्रीरामाय नमः ॐ —

Ignorance is not merely a lack of information; it is a primordial veiling of the true Self—causing the bound soul (jīva) to mistake the unreal for the real, the perishable for the eternal, the body for the Self.

As long as this veiling persists, beings are caught in bondage, confusion, and sorrow.

But when ज्ञान jñāna arises through discipline, inquiry, and grace, it shines like the sun—revealing the Self, not as a distant object, but as the very essence of one's being.

This verse thus celebrates the liberating power of true knowledge and the end of delusion for the awakened sage.

—: Key Sanskrit Terms :—

Let us trace the golden threads of the verse's meaning by lingering with its luminous Sanskrit gems, each a doorway to deeper realms. Let the Sanskrit words rise—like sunrise dissolving the night.

When the wisdom of Gitā illumines, then ignorance vanishes and things begin to shine like the sun. Each syllable here is a new dawn that awakens human heart.

— ॐ —

ज्ञानेन तु तदज्ञानं (Jñānena tu tadajñānaṁ):

Here, ज्ञान jñāna — the light of Self-knowledge — is the fire that burns away अज्ञान ajñāna — ignorance, the primal cause of delusion and bondage.

It is not by mere ritual, nor by external disciplines alone, but by the luminous awakening of inner knowledge that the darkness of mind is dispelled.

— ॐ —

येषां नाशितम् आत्मनः (Yeṣāṁ nāśitam ātmanaḥ):

नाशितम् Nāśitam — "destroyed" — indicates the complete dissolution of the veil of ignorance covering the Self (Ātmā).

For such beings, the Self no longer appears hidden or separate, but shines forth in its native splendor.

— ॐ —

तेषाम् आदित्यवत् ज्ञानम् (Teṣām ādityavat jñānam):

For these purified souls, jñāna — their knowledge — becomes like the आदित्य āditya — the radiant sun.

Just as the sun, by its mere presence, reveals the whole world without effort, so too Self-knowledge reveals the nature of Reality effortlessly, fully, and unmistakably.

— ॐ —

प्रकाशयति तत्परम् (Prakāśayati tatparam):

प्रकाशयति Prakāśayati — "illuminates" — तत्परम् tat-param — "That Supreme Reality." It is not a partial revelation, but a complete shining forth of the Infinite (Braham), where no shadow of doubt remains.

See how every word beautifully portrays the inner dawn when ignorance vanishes and the eternal, limitless Self is realized.

From man to God—what a luminous transformation indeed.

—: In Brief :—

— ॐ श्रीकृष्णरामाभ्यां नमः ॐ —

Shri Krishna, having just spoken of the soul's delusion in the previous verse, now declares the remedy: the blazing light of Self-knowledge that annihilates ignorance entirely.

The analogy is vivid and sublime: "Just as the sun, rising, dispels darkness and reveals the world as it truly is, so too does jñāna, when arisen, dispel the darkness of ajñāna and reveal the Self—all the way to the Supreme."

— ॐ योगीश्वराय नमः ॐ —

Here, the sun सूर्यः (sūryaḥ) represents pure, unwavering knowledge—free from distortion or duality.

Just as light is not an added property of the sun but its very nature, so too is jñāna not an external acquisition for the Self, but the uncovering of what was always inherently present.

Mind it, the illumination mentioned here in this verse, extends not just to worldly understanding, but to the highest state—the direct vision of Braham, the Absolute.

Hence, knowledge is not a means to an end—it is the end, for it is identical with liberation (mokṣa).

— ॐ श्रीरामाय नमः ॐ —

The phrase तत्परम् tatparam —"that supreme", or "that being"—points unmistakably toward Parama-Puruṣa, the Supreme Reality, which becomes clearly known when the veil of ignorance is lifted.

The knower then does not merely understand God as a concept, but abides in the vision of the Divine as the Self of all.

This transformation is not partial or temporary. When true knowledge arises, the delusion that once clouded perception is not merely suppressed—it is completely burned away, like mist before the morning sun.

Now the jīva no longer identifies with the body-mind complex but recognizes itself as सत-चित-आनन्द sat-cit-ānanda—existence-bliss-consciousness.

— ॐ चिरंजीविने नमः ॐ —

In this way, Shri Krishna distinguishes the realized sage (jñānī) from the deluded beings spoken of in verse 15. The key difference lies not in external behavior but in vision—what one sees and knows oneself to be.

This verse also alludes to the fruits of Sāṅkhya-Yoga, the path of discrimination and contemplation. It is through resolute inquiry into the nature of the Self and sustained abidance in its Truth that ignorance is dissolved and freedom attained.

With this, Bhagwāna Shri Krishna moves from describing ignorance and its consequences to extolling the supreme transformation brought about by Self-realization. The next verse will continue to describe the liberated ones—who dwell in that light, free from bondage, seeing the One in all and all in the One.

— ॐ तत सत ॐ —

Before moving on, let us once more bow in deep reverence before this sacred verse of the Bhagavad-Gītā, an eternal beacon of wisdom that ceaselessly illumines the path of seekers. Engage with its form—inscribe it with your own hand, let your heart dwell upon its meaning, and raise your voice in its chanting—for within these syllables echoes the undying proclamation delivered millennia ago on the battlefield of Kurukshetra. These words, transmitted unchanged across the unbroken chain of generations, form a living bridge, linking us to that sanctified era when Bhagwāna Shri Krishna Himself walked this earth and bestowed this divine teaching. Through the luminous vibration of these sacred Sanskrit sounds, we are drawn nearer to His timeless presence, touching the very heartbeat of the Eternal.

— ॐ —

ज्ञानेन तु तदज्ञानं येषां नाशितमात्मनः ।
jñānena tu tadajñānaṁ yeṣāṁ nāśitamātmanaḥ
तेषामादित्यवज्ज्ञानं प्रकाशयति तत्परम् ॥५-१६॥
teṣāmādityavajjñānaṁ prakāśayati tatparam (5-16)

— ॐ —

ज्ञानेन तु तदज्ञानं येषां नाशितमात्मनः ।
jñānena tu tadajñānaṁ yeṣāṁ nāśitamātmanaḥ
तेषामादित्यवज्ज्ञानं प्रकाशयति तत्परम् ॥५-१६॥
teṣāmādityavajjñānaṁ prakāśayati tatparam (5-16)

ॐ तत्सदिति श्रीमद्भगवद्गीतासूपनिषत्सु ब्रह्मविद्यायां योगशास्त्रे श्रीकृष्णार्जुनसंवादे
om tatsaditi śrīmadbhagavadgītāsūpaniṣatsu brahmavidyāyāṁ yogaśāstre śrīkṛṣṇārjunasaṁvāde
संन्यासयोगो नाम पञ्चमोऽध्यायः श्लोकः १६
saṁnyāsayogo nāma pañcamo'dhyāyaḥ ślokaḥ 16

Om-Tat-Sat—Om (Braham) is the sole Reality. In the Yogic Scripture on the Science-of-Braham, the Shrimada-Bhāgvada-Gītā Upanishad, we hereby conclude Shloka 16 of the Dialogue between Shrī Krishna and Arjuna entitled Sanyāsa-Yoga, Canto V.

— ॐ कोदण्डधारिणे नमः ॐ —

In Days of Yore in Aryavarta, the Birth-Land of Civilization,
The mind was made to reflect inwards.
But today's fool abandoned Sanātana-Dharma—turned his mind fully out.

—o—

Now he mistakes the mirage of colored mirrors to be Light.
The sun still shines—but he has fallen in love with sparkling neon.
He gropes in night with a broken torch.
Keeps swiping at screens. Feeding on inanities. Imbibing trivia.
Munching on corn,
Hollering with the crowds, counting likes & stars,
Unknown to the real earth, moon, sun, stars,
Reeling on reels,
The only thing he fears is: the Quiet.

O fool—befriend the Quiet.
For Quiet is inevitable when one day ye die.
None of this glitter will come to thy rescue at then.
O fool, have thou heard of the Realm of Bliss that's right inside thee—
where all sounds become quiet,
and all lights fade into the oneness of satt-chitt-ānanda braham.

ॐ गीता श्लोकः ५.१७ – GĪTĀ VERSE 5.17

ॐ श्रीमद्भगवद्गीतासूपनिषत्सु ब्रह्मविद्यायां योगशास्त्रे श्रीकृष्णार्जुनसंवादे
om śrīmadbhagavadgītāsūpaniṣatsu brahmavidyāyāṁ yogaśāstre śrīkṛṣṇārjunasaṁvāde
संन्यासयोगो नाम पञ्चमोऽध्यायः श्लोकः १७
saṁnyāsayogo nāma pañcamo'dhyāyaḥ ślokaḥ 17

— ॐ —

तद्बुद्धयस्तदात्मानस्तन्निष्ठास्तत्परायणाः ।
tadbuddhayastadātmānastanniṣṭhāstatparāyaṇāḥ
गच्छन्त्यपुनरावृत्तिं ज्ञाननिर्धूतकल्मषाः ॥५-१७॥
gacchantyapunarāvṛttiṁ jñānanirdhūtakalmaṣāḥ (5-17)

With his sins winnowed away through knowledge he—who is decided upon Him, who has his heart and mind fixed upon Him, who is devoted to Him, who has Him alone as his ultimate refuge—reaches that Supreme-Abode wherefrom there is no return to this world of sorrows. (5.17)

—: *Word-by-Word* :—

तत् बुद्धयः tad-buddhayaḥ – those whose intellect is absorbed in That; तत् आत्मानः tad-ātmānaḥ – those whose self is absorbed in That; तत् निष्ठाः tad-niṣṭhāḥ – those steadfast in That; तत् परायणाः tat-parāyaṇāḥ – those who take That as the supreme goal; गच्छन्ति gacchanti – go; अपुनरावृत्तिम् apunarāvṛttim – to non-return (liberation); ज्ञाननिर्धूतकल्मषाः jñāna-nirdhūta-kalmaṣāḥ – with impurities dispelled by knowledge.

—: *Understanding The Verse* :—

— ॐ श्रीकृष्णाय नमः ॐ —

In this sublime verse, Bhagwāna Shri Krishna declares the supreme culmination of spiritual striving—God-realization—attained by those who have thoroughly purified their minds through Self-knowledge.

This verse reveals the inner state of those whose understanding बुद्धि (buddhi), attention मानस् (manas), devotion भक्ति (bhakti), and ultimate refuge परायण (parāyaṇa) are all wholly directed toward the Supreme Reality, referred to here as तत Tat—That Absolute, Braham.

— ॐ श्रीरामाय नमः ॐ —

These seekers are not just intellectual aspirants—they are those who have merged their entire being into the contemplation and realization of the Truth Absolute, identified with सच्चिदानन्द

Saccidānanda—Existence, Consciousness, and Bliss. A very high state indeed.

Their impurities कल्मष (kalmasha)—the subtle residues of past karma, desires, prejudices, and delusions—have been entirely consumed in the fire of true knowledge (jñāna).

Such souls reach the Supreme Abode परमगतिः(param gatiḥ), which is final, beyond return, free from the cycle of becoming.

Thus, this verse beautifully brings together the themes of devotion, wisdom, purification, and liberation, showing that realization of Braham is not partial or symbolic—it is the total transformation of being.

—: Key Sanskrit Terms :—

Let us wander the delicate waterways of the verse, where each Sanskrit word is like a river converging into the sea—unfurling swirls of hidden wisdom wherever the twain meet.

"Fixing mind and soul on Him, purified by wisdom, the yogi reaches that realm from where there is no more return to this world of sorrows." Each word merges, endless, into vastness.

— ॐ —

तद्बुद्धयः (Tadbuddhayaḥ): Those whose intellect बुद्धि (buddhi) is absorbed into That, तत tat — the Supreme.

The mind that was once scattered among myriad worldly aims becomes fully gathered and fixed upon the Eternal—perceiving Him alone as the goal, the aim of human life—for all life and existence is just from Him.

— ॐ —

तदात्मानः (Tadātmānaḥ): Their very being आत्मानः (Ātmānḥ) is merged in तद् That.

The jīva, ceasing to identify with body and mind, identifies solely with Braham, recognizing no difference between Self and the Supreme.

— ॐ —

तन्निष्ठाः (Tanniṣṭhāḥ): They are firmly rooted निष्ठ (niṣṭhā) in That alone, unwavering, immovable.

Their entire life, thought, and endeavor are anchored in the immutable Reality, like a tree whose roots are buried deep in fertile soil.

— ॐ —

तत्परायणाः (Tatparāyaṇāḥ): They have taken refuge परायण (parāyaṇa) exclusively in That Supreme.

They seek no other support, no other fulfillment; their devotion and surrender are complete.

— ॐ —

ज्ञाननिर्धूतकल्मषाः (Jñānanirdhūtakalmaṣāḥ): Through the fire of knowledge ज्ञान (jñāna), all stains of sin कल्मष (kalmaṣa) have been निर्धूत nirdhūta — completely burnt away.

Ignorance and its offspring — desire, fear, sorrow — are dissolved, leaving the soul pure and luminous.

— ॐ —

गच्छन्ति अपुनरावृत्तिं (Gacchanti apunarāvṛttim): Such souls ascend गच्छन्ति (gacchanti) to the Supreme state (tat param), from which there is अपुनरावृत्तिं apunaraāvṛtti — no return to mortal existence, no fall back into the cycle of birth and death संसार (saṁsāra).

The entirety of this majestic verse conveys the glorious culmination of spiritual striving — absorption into the Eternal, freedom from all bondages.

—: In Brief :—

— ॐ श्रीकृष्णाय नमः ॐ —

Shri Krishna, having previously spoken of the illumination that arises when ignorance is dispelled (5.16), now describes the state of those who live in that illumination made firm—whose vision is fixed on the Supreme, whose very essence is saturated with Self-knowledge.

— ॐ श्रीरामाय नमः ॐ —

The phrase "तत् बुद्धयः tadbuddhayaḥ" denotes those whose intellect is rooted in That तत् (tat)—the Supreme Being.

Their understanding no longer moves within the domain of the fleeting or the fragmented. It is steadfast in the vision of the Eternal.

"तत् निष्ठाः Tannishṭhāḥ" means that their very stance—mental, moral, and spiritual—is grounded in That Reality.

They do not waver between the transient and the timeless; their entire life is anchored in the Infinite.

— ॐ बालकृष्णाय नमः ॐ —

"ज्ञाननिर्धूतकल्मषाः jñāna-nirdhūta-kalmaṣāḥ —the sins (kalmasha) that once veiled their vision are no more. These "sins" are not merely moral faults, but the obscurations of perception: distraction, egoism, prejudice, restlessness, and forgetfulness of the Self.

True knowledge (jñāna) here is not a philosophical concept, but a direct and transformative vision that consumes these impurities like fire burns away dross.

Such souls, says Shri Krishna, attain "अपुनरावृत्तिम् apunarāvṛttim"—that state from which there is no return. They reach the Supreme Goal, not as a distant realm but as the ever-present Reality, now known, seen, and lived as the very Self.

Just as a man, once awakened from dream, never returns to identify with the illusions of his sleep, so too the liberated one never returns to the entanglements of ignorance and karma.

— ॐ परिपूर्णतमाय नमः ॐ —

This verse concludes a major thematic arc of the fifth chapter: the reconciliation of renunciation and action, of wisdom and devotion, and the culmination of both in liberation from rebirth.

The Gītā now prepares to take us deeper into the vision of the wise, the seers of unity, and those who see the One in all beings and all beings in the One.

— ॐ तत सत ॐ —

Before we move on, let us bow in reverence to this sacred verse. Write it by hand, reflect on its meaning, chant it aloud, make it your own.

— ॐ —

तद्बुद्धयस्तदात्मानस्तन्निष्ठास्तत्परायणाः ।
tadbuddhayastadātmānastanniṣṭhāstatparāyaṇāḥ
गच्छन्त्यपुनरावृत्तिं ज्ञाननिर्धूतकल्मषाः ॥५-१७॥
gacchantyapunarāvṛttiṁ jñānanirdhūtakalmaṣāḥ (5-17)

— ॐ —

तद्बुद्धयस्तदात्मानस्तन्निष्ठास्तत्परायणाः ।
tadbuddhayastadātmānastanniṣṭhāstatparāyaṇāḥ
गच्छन्त्यपुनरावृत्तिं ज्ञाननिर्धूतकल्मषाः ॥५-१७॥
gacchantyapunarāvṛttiṁ jñānanirdhūtakalmaṣāḥ (5-17)

ॐ तत्सदिति श्रीमद्भगवद्गीतासूपनिषत्सु ब्रह्मविद्यायां योगशास्त्रे श्रीकृष्णार्जुनसंवादे
om tatsaditi śrīmadbhagavadgītāsūpaniṣatsu brahmavidyāyāṁ yogaśāstre śrīkṛṣṇārjunasaṁvāde
संन्यासयोगो नाम पञ्चमोऽध्यायः श्लोकः १७
saṁnyāsayogo nāma pañcamo'dhyāyaḥ ślokaḥ 17

Om-Tat-Sat—Om (Braham) is the sole Reality. In the Yogic Scripture on the Science-of-Braham, the Shrimada-Bhāgvada-Gītā Upanishad, we hereby conclude Shloka 17 of the Dialogue between Shrī Krishna and Arjuna entitled Sanyāsa-Yoga, Canto V.

ॐ गीता श्लोकः ५.१८ – GĪTĀ VERSE 5.18

ॐ श्रीमद्भगवद्गीतासूपनिषत्सु ब्रह्मविद्यायां योगशास्त्रे श्रीकृष्णार्जुनसंवादे
om śrīmadbhagavadgītāsūpaniṣatsu brahmavidyāyāṁ yogaśāstre śrīkṛṣṇārjunasaṁvāde
संन्यासयोगो नाम पञ्चमोऽध्यायः श्लोकः १८
saṁnyāsayogo nāma pañcamo'dhyāyaḥ ślokaḥ 18

— ॐ —

विद्याविनयसम्पन्ने ब्राह्मणे गवि हस्तिनि ।
vidyāvinayasampanne brāhmaṇe gavi hastini
शुनि चैव श्वपाके च पण्डिताः समदर्शिनः ॥५-१८॥
śuni caiva śvapāke ca paṇḍitāḥ samadarśinaḥ (5-18)

The wise looks upon all beings with an equable eye—whether it be a Brahmin endowed with humility and learning, or a pariah, or a cow, or an elephant, or a dog. (5.18)

—: Word-by-Word :—

विद्याविनयसम्पन्ने vidyā-vinaya-sampanne – endowed with knowledge and humility; ब्राह्मणे brāhmaṇe – in a Brahmin; गवि gavi – in a cow; हस्तिनि hastini – in an elephant; शुनि śuni – in a dog; च eva – and also; श्वपाके śvapāke – in an outcaste; पण्डिताः paṇḍitāḥ – the wise; समदर्शिनः samadarśinaḥ – see with equal vision.

—: Understanding The Verse :—

— ॐ श्रीकृष्णाय नमः ॐ —

In this verse, Bhagwāna Shri Krishna offers a luminous portrait of the wise one पण्डिताः (pañḍitaḥ)—the sage who has realized the Self and therefore sees all beings with equanimity.

From the exalted ब्राह्मण Brahmin, adorned with humility and wisdom, to the lowly श्वपाक śvapāka (dog-eater), from the noble elephant to the humble dog or cow—the Self-realized soul sees no essential distinction.

— ॐ श्रीरामाय नमः ॐ —

This vision arises not from superficial sentiment but from the profound insight into the unity that pervades all diversity. The sage has pierced through the veil of names and forms नाम रुप (nāma-rūpa) and recognizes the One Imperishable Consciousness dwelling equally in all beings.

Thus, while the external forms vary in quality, capacity, and social role, the indwelling Reality (Ātmā or Braham) remains the same.

This verse illustrates the fruits of Self-realization: an unwavering vision of oneness amidst multiplicity, which is the hallmark of the liberated soul.

—: Key Sanskrit Terms :—

Let us draw back the veil of this verse, guided by the shimmering light of its key Sanskrit terms, each revealing of unseen horizons. Each syllable here dissolves differences into a single light—as with a sage's gaze steady and equal. Cow, elephant, dog, outcaste—the wise sees all with the vision of sameness.

— ॐ —

विद्याविनयसम्पन्ने ब्राह्मणे (Vidyāvinayasampanne brāhmaṇe):

The ब्राह्मण brāhmaṇa referred to here is not merely one by birth, but one सम्पन्न sampanna — endowed with विद्या vidyā (true knowledge) and विनय vinaya (humility).

Learning without humility is incomplete; together they form the true ornament of wisdom.

— ॐ —

गवि हस्तिनि (Gavi hastini):

The cow गवि (gavi) and the elephant हस्तिनि (hastini) represent beings of vastly different capacities and temperaments, yet the wise sees beyond outer form into the one animating Spirit that pervades all.

— ॐ —

शुनि च एव श्वपाके च (Śuni caiva śvapāke ca):

The dog शुनि (śuni) and the श्वपाक śvapāka (one who cooks and eats dog meat, symbolizing an outcaste) represent beings often despised by society. Yet to the truly wise, distinctions of high and low are but appearances; the indwelling Self is equal in all.

— ॐ —

पण्डिताः समदर्शिनः (Paṇḍitāḥ samadarśinaḥ):

The पण्डिताः paṇḍitaḥ — the truly wise — are समदर्शिनः samadarśinaḥ, seeing with equal vision. सम दर्शन Sama-darśana is not superficial equality but the deep perception of the आत्मा Ātmā shining equally through all coverings, whether noble or humble.

Thus, every phrase of this श्लोक śloka opens the gateway to a vision beyond form, caste, or species — into the pure light of oneness.

—: *In Brief* :—

— ॐ श्रीकृष्णाय नमः ॐ —

In this profound and poetically inclusive verse, Shri Krishna declares: "**विद्याविनयसम्पन्ने ब्राह्मणे** ... Vidya-vinaya-sampanne brāhmaṇe..."—the wise see the same Reality in all.

The term **पण्डिताः** paṇḍitāḥ does not refer to mere scholars of scriptural lore, but to those ennobled by wisdom and purified by direct realization.

These are the ones whose inner vision has been cleared of all delusions, who no longer identify with external distinctions of form, function, birth, or species.

— ॐ श्रीरामाय नमः ॐ —

The examples given—a humble and learned Brahmin, a cow, an elephant, a dog, and a dog-eater—are purposefully varied. They represent the spectrum of created beings across the axes of purity, utility, intelligence, and social status. Yet, the sage sees the same Self shining in all—like one sun reflected in many waters.

This **समदर्शिन** sama-darśin—one who sees equally—is not naïvely blind to outer distinctions, but inwardly free of attachment to them.

— ॐ समुद्रशरणागतवत्सलाय नमः ॐ —

Indeed, the realized one does not live in denial of social or practical realities. He very much observes the necessary distinctions in behavior, as prescribed by Dharma—a Brahmin may be worshipped, a pariah not; a cow may give nourishing milk, a dog may not. An elephant may be majestic, yet must be approached cautiously.

But inwardly, the sage holds equal reverence for all, knowing that in all forms, it is Braham alone who resides—though this vision cannot be outwardly expressed in practice so long as the body stays draped and one must stay bound to societal norms.

— ॐ वरप्रदाय नमः ॐ —

But once death is upon us, and the body is about to fall off—it is best to hold on to that vision of oneness and of nothing else—perceiving just only Braham throughout the cosmos, without any differentiations at all.

Let all forms and names be gone now, let all relatives, friends, friend, foe, wealth, house forever disappear—just only satt-chitt-ānanda braham, the ocean of existence-bliss-consciousness, whose manifest form is Bhagwāna Shri Krishna should remain at then.

— ॐ वन्दे सूर्य शशाङ्क वह्निनयन वन्दे मुकुन्द प्रियम् ॐ —

But returning to the vision of oneness in practice, the scriptures often compare this vision to how one regards different limbs of one's own body: the head is held in high esteem, the feet are not; yet both are part of the same whole, and one feels pain equally if either is harmed. Likewise, the sage, though interacting appropriately according to context, remains inwardly unified in love, compassion, and equanimity, for he sees none as other.

— ॐ श्रीनिधये नमः ॐ —

Such a vision is not theoretical, but arises from the complete dissolution of the ego and the realization of one's identity with the परमात्मा Paramātman. For this sage, the world is not a collection of others, but manifestations of the One. This is the vision of unity एकत्व दर्शन (ekatva-darśana) that is the essence of Vedānta and the fruit of profound meditation and Self-knowledge.

— ॐ वेदात्मने नमः ॐ —

This verse serves not merely as an ethical teaching, but as a metaphysical revelation: true equality is possible only when the Self is known. Without that knowledge, all attempts at moral or social equality remain partial and external.

As we find in the isavasyopanishad, unto the jñānī, the entire world is pervaded by God : ईशा वास्यमिदᳪ सर्वं यत्किञ्च जगत्यां जगत् (īśā vāsyamidaṁ sarvaṁ yatkiñca jagatyāṁ jagat), and every being is a doorway to the Divine.

Having revealed this vision of the sage, Shri Krishna now prepares to describe in the following verses the fruit of this realization—a state of peace, unshakeable equanimity, and absorption in the Supreme.

— ॐ तत सत ॐ —

Before we move on, let us bow in reverence to this sacred verse—a timeless beacon of wisdom guiding seekers for ages. Write it by hand, reflect on its meaning, and chant it aloud, for these sounds alone carry the authenticity of that era. The world may have changed but the living vibration of these Sanskrit sounds still remain as original as they were when Bhagwān Shri Krishna Himself walked the earth and imparted these teachings.

— ॐ —

विद्याविनयसम्पन्ने ब्राह्मणे गवि हस्तिनि ।
vidyāvinayasampanne brāhmaṇe gavi hastini
शुनि चैव श्वपाके च पण्डिताः समदर्शिनः ॥५-१८॥
śuni caiva śvapāke ca paṇḍitāḥ samadarśinaḥ (5-18)

ॐ

विद्याविनयसम्पन्ने ब्राह्मणे गवि हस्तिनि ।
vidyāvinayasampanne brāhmaṇe gavi hastini
शुनि चैव श्वपाके च पण्डिताः समदर्शिनः ॥५-१८॥
śuni caiva śvapāke ca paṇḍitāḥ samadarśinaḥ (5-18)

ॐ तत्सदिति श्रीमद्भगवद्गीतासूपनिषत्सु ब्रह्मविद्यायां योगशास्त्रे श्रीकृष्णार्जुनसंवादे
om tatsaditi śrīmadbhagavadgītāsūpaniṣatsu brahmavidyāyāṁ yogaśāstre śrīkṛṣṇārjunasaṁvāde
संन्यासयोगो नाम पञ्चमोऽध्यायः श्लोकः १८
saṁnyāsayogo nāma pañcamo'dhyāyaḥ ślokaḥ 18

Om-Tat-Sat—Om (Braham) is the sole Reality. In the Yogic Scripture on the Science-of-Braham, the Shrimada-Bhāgvada-Gītā Upanishad, we hereby conclude Shloka 18 of the Dialogue between Shrī Krishna and Arjuna entitled Sanyāsa-Yoga, Canto V.

— ॐ श्रीकृष्णाय नमः ॐ —

The Sky Always Stays As Itself—Beyond All Weathers
Whatever clouds may cry, what winds may rage,
what suns may blaze or darkness pour—
The space, eternal, bears them all—
yet changeth not its silent core,

So too the one whose mind is firm,
whose sight is yoked to Self alone,
Feels not the prick of joy or grief—nor heeds the storm that mortals own.
To him, all gain is but a wave,
all loss a ripple, faint and dim,
And thus he dwells in evenness—
like lotus blooming o'er the brim.

The Karma-Yogi abides in a world where things do flux, things do sway,
yet he remains untouched —
unmoved by gold, skin, clay; fame, praise, blame.

In the cave of his heart, a light shines—
not lit by oil, nor fed by flame.
It does not burn; it simply is—
self-luminous, serene, without beginning or end.

The Yogi knows himself as the sky, which ever stays whole—
Even though winds will shatter the cloud below.
Beyond the body, the yogi knows he is the eternal ātmā —
Consciousness pure, radiant only in his beingness.

ॐ गीता श्लोकः ५.१९ – GĪTĀ VERSE 5.19

ॐ श्रीमद्भगवद्गीतासूपनिषत्सु ब्रह्मविद्यायां योगशास्त्रे श्रीकृष्णार्जुनसंवादे
om śrīmadbhagavadgītāsūpaniṣatsu brahmavidyāyāṁ yogaśāstre śrīkṛṣṇārjunasaṁvāde
संन्यासयोगो नाम पञ्चमोऽध्यायः श्लोकः १९
saṁnyāsayogo nāma pañcamo'dhyāyaḥ ślokaḥ 19

— ॐ —

इहैव तैर्जितः सर्गो येषां साम्ये स्थितं मनः ।
ihaiva tairjitaḥ sargo yeṣāṁ sāmye sthitaṁ manaḥ
निर्दोषं हि समं ब्रह्म तस्माद् ब्रह्मणि ते स्थिताः ॥५-१९॥
nirdoṣaṁ hi samaṁ brahma tasmād brahmaṇi te sthitāḥ (5-19)

Even this here mortal plane stands conquered by those whose minds stand established in sameness and equanimity. The Absolute Being is untouched by evil and is the same to all—hence they stand established in That Brahama.
(5.19)

—: *Word-by-Word* :—

इह eva ihaiva – here itself; तैः taiḥ – by them; जितः jitah – is conquered; सर्गः sargaḥ – creation (rebirth); येषाम् yeṣām – whose; साम्ये sāmye – in equanimity; स्थितम् sthitam – is established; मनः manaḥ – mind; निर्दोषम् nirdoṣam – faultless; हि hi – indeed; समम् samam – equal; ब्रह्म brahma – Braham; तस्मात् tasmāt – therefore; ब्रह्मणि brahmaṇi – in Braham; ते te – they; स्थिताः sthitāḥ – are established.

—: *Understanding The Verse* :—

— ॐ श्रीकृष्णाय नमः ॐ —

In this verse, Bhagwāna Shri Krishna declares the spiritual triumph of those whose minds are firmly established in sameness, in the vision of unity. Such sages, even while living in the body and moving in the world, have conquered the mortal condition—they are no longer bound by the limitations of body, mind, circumstance.

Their victory lies in the transcendence of dualities, which are born of contact with प्रकृति Prakṛti and its three गुण guṇas—sattva, rajas, and tamas. These wise ones see no essential division, no separation, and no otherness. Their mind no longer clings to likes and dislikes, gain and loss, honor and dishonor.

Because Braham, the Supreme Reality, is untouched by all such dualities and distinctions, the ones who live in ब्रह्म भाव Braham-bhāva—a state of identity with Braham—are likewise pure, equal-minded, and freed from all blemish. Their realization is not in words or thoughts alone, but in the deep absorption of the heart and mind into the Formless Absolute.

—: Key Sanskrit Terms :—

Let us now listen closely to the verse's heartbeat, as its core Sanskrit expressions whisper secrets of profound depths to us. They talk of chains breaking in silence. Unbinding knot after knot, each word frees. The even-minded conquer birth and death, dwelling ever in Braham.

— ॐ —

इहैव तैः जितः सर्गः (Ihaiva taiḥ jitaḥ sargaḥ):
Here इहैव (ihaiva), even while living in this mortal realm,
सर्गः sargaḥ — the creation, the binding cycle of birth and death — is
जितः jitaḥ — conquered — by those whose vision has become clear.
Liberation is not a far-off heavenly attainment but a realization here and now for the soul who knows.

— ॐ —

येषां साम्ये स्थितं मनः (Yeṣāṁ sāmye sthitaṁ manaḥ):
Those whose minds मानस् (manas) are स्थितं sthitaṁ — firmly established — in साम्य sāmya — perfect equanimity and sameness.
Their gaze no longer wavers amidst dualities; they see with even vision, unmoved by pleasure or pain, praise or blame, high or low.

— ॐ —

निर्दोषं हि समं ब्रह्म (Nirdoṣaṁ hi samaṁ brahma):
Braham — the Supreme Reality — is निर्दोषं nirdoṣaṁ — flawless, without any taint or blemish — and समं samaṁ — equal in all beings and all forms.
He is beyond virtue and vice, untouched by dualities, shining with unconditioned purity.

— ॐ —

तस्मात् ब्रह्मणि ते स्थिताः (Tasmād brahmaṇi te sthitāḥ):
Therefore तस्मात् (tasmāt), those who have conquered सर्ग sarga through equanimity are स्थिताः sthitāḥ — firmly established — in Braham itself.
Their being is no longer tossed upon the waves of प्रकृति prakṛti; they abide immovable in the infinite Light.

Every term here has brought forth a grand vision: the conquest of the world not by force, but by stillness; not by fleeing life, but by realizing the Eternal within life.

—: In Brief :—

— ॐ श्रीकृष्णाय नमः ॐ —

Shri Krishna here proclaims that इहैव "Even here"—in this mortal world, in the very midst of embodied life—the wise who are established in equanimity have already conquered death, which means they have transcended the bondage of birth and rebirth.

The key lies in साम्ये sāmye – in equanimity—those whose understanding is established in sameness, in oneness with all beings.

These seers have pierced through the illusion of division and perceive Braham equally present in saint and sinner, in joy and sorrow, in high and low.

Their inner instrument अन्तः करण (antaḥkaraṇa) has become tranquil and mirror-like, reflecting only the non-dual Truth.

— ॐ श्रीरामाय नमः ॐ —

The Gītā does not preach a naïve leveling of all distinctions in outer conduct; rather, it speaks of an inner realization that transcends diversity without denying it. These sages move in the world, yet are untouched by it—like the lotus that floats upon water yet is never wetted by it.

Why are they no longer bound by the world of becoming संसार (saṁsāra)? Because they stay established in Braham—"ब्रह्मणि ते स्थिताः brahmaṇi te sthitāḥ".

Braham is nirguṇa—free from the three qualities (guṇas) of Nature. While sattva, rajas, and tamas shape all phenomena, Braham remains beyond them—eternal, unchanging, untouched by good or evil, pure or impure.

— ॐ परमानन्दाय नमः ॐ —

Those who have truly realized Braham must themselves be free of these guṇas, including even sattva eventually, which, though noble and luminous, still binds the soul through attachment to knowledge and joy. As Shri Krishna later teaches (in Chapter 14), eventually even sattva must be transcended in order to enter perfect freedom गुणातीत (guṇātīta).

It is for this reason—having gone beyond the guṇas—that the sage is said to have conquered the mortal plane. Though the body still lives, eats, and moves, the sense of separate identity is gone. Though the world appears, it no longer binds. This is not escape from the world, but supreme transcendence while within it.

— ॐ आर्याय नमः ॐ —

Furthermore, the sage's unity is not passive neutrality—it is divine love and inclusiveness born of recognition.

Just as one sees all limbs of the body as one's own, so too the sage sees the whole world as his very Self. He is not indifferent but equally responsive, rooted in the stillness of Braham.

In the next verse, Shri Krishna continues to describe this exalted one, who has become ब्रह्मणि स्थितः brahmaṇi sthitaḥ —one with the Absolute—whose delight is no longer in the transient, but in the eternal.

— ॐ तत सत ॐ —

Before we move on, let us bow in reverence to this sacred verse—a timeless beacon of wisdom guiding seekers for ages. Write it by hand, reflect on its meaning, and chant it aloud, for these sounds alone carry the authenticity of that era. The world may have changed but the living vibration of these Sanskrit sounds still remain as original as they were when Bhagwān Shri Krishna Himself walked the earth and imparted these teachings.

— ॐ —

इहैव तैर्जितः सर्गो येषां साम्ये स्थितं मनः ।
ihaiva tairjitaḥ sargo yeṣāṁ sāmye sthitaṁ manaḥ
निर्दोषं हि समं ब्रह्म तस्माद् ब्रह्मणि ते स्थिताः ॥५-१९॥
nirdoṣaṁ hi samaṁ brahma tasmād brahmaṇi te sthitāḥ (5-19)

— ॐ —

इहैव तैर्जितः सर्गो येषां साम्ये स्थितं मनः ।
ihaiva tairjitaḥ sargo yeṣāṁ sāmye sthitaṁ manaḥ
निर्दोषं हि समं ब्रह्म तस्माद् ब्रह्मणि ते स्थिताः ॥५-१९॥
nirdoṣaṁ hi samaṁ brahma tasmād brahmaṇi te sthitāḥ (5-19)

ॐ तत्सदिति श्रीमद्भगवद्गीतासूपनिषत्सु ब्रह्मविद्यायां योगशास्त्रे श्रीकृष्णार्जुनसंवादे
om tatsaditi śrīmadbhagavadgītāsūpaniṣatsu brahmavidyāyāṁ yogaśāstre śrīkṛṣṇārjunasaṁvāde
संन्यासयोगो नाम पञ्चमोऽध्यायः श्लोकः १९
saṁnyāsayogo nāma pañcamo'dhyāyaḥ ślokaḥ 19

Om-Tat-Sat—Om (Braham) is the sole Reality. In the Yogic Scripture on the Science-of-Braham, the Shrimada-Bhāgvada-Gītā Upanishad, we hereby conclude Shloka 19 of the Dialogue between Shrī Krishna and Arjuna entitled Sanyāsa-Yoga, Canto V.

ॐ गीता श्लोकः ५.२० – GĪTĀ VERSE 5.20

ॐ श्रीमद्भगवद्गीतासूपनिषत्सु ब्रह्मविद्यायां योगशास्त्रे श्रीकृष्णार्जुनसंवादे
om śrīmadbhagavadgītāsūpaniṣatsu brahmavidyāyāṁ yogaśāstre śrīkṛṣṇārjunasaṁvāde
संन्यासयोगो नाम पञ्चमोऽध्यायः श्लोकः २०
saṁnyāsayogo nāma pañcamo'dhyāyaḥ ślokaḥ 20

— ॐ —

न प्रहृष्येत्प्रियं प्राप्य नोद्विजेत्प्राप्य चाप्रियम् ।
na prahṛṣyetpriyaṁ prāpya nodvijetprāpya cāpriyam
स्थिरबुद्धिरसम्मूढो ब्रह्मविद् ब्रह्मणि स्थितः ॥५-२०॥
sthirabuddhirasammūḍho brahmavid brahmaṇi sthitaḥ (5-20)

The Knower of Brahama—firm of mind, free of doubts, who lives established in Brahama—is not elated upon obtaining the sweet, nor gets perturbed upon begetting the bitter. (5.20)

—: Word-by-Word :—

न na – neither; प्रहृष्येत् prahṛṣyet – should rejoice; प्रियं priyam – in the pleasant; प्राप्य prāpya – upon obtaining; न na – nor; उद्विजेत् udvijet – be agitated; प्राप्य prāpya – upon obtaining; च ca – and; अप्रियम apriyam – the unpleasant; स्थिरबुद्धिः sthira-buddhiḥ – with steady intellect; असम्मूढः asammūḍhaḥ – undeluded; ब्रह्मविद् brahmavid – the knower of Braham; ब्रह्मणि brahmaṇi – in Braham; स्थितः sthitaḥ – established.

—: Understanding The Verse :—

— ॐ श्रीकृष्णाय नमः ॐ —

In this verse, Bhagwāna Shri Krishna describes the unwavering serenity and inner equipoise of the knower of Braham—the one who has realized the Self as identical with the Supreme Reality. Such a realized one is firm in intellect, free from delusion, and unshaken by the dualities of life.

The verse emphasizes that one who abides in Braham does not become elated by the pleasurable nor disturbed by the painful. His inner state is not contingent on external events, for his awareness is rooted in That which is beyond all conditions—the formless, immutable Braham.

This sublime equanimity is not a cultivated indifference but arises spontaneously from the direct realization that the world of opposites is illusory and impermanent.

Thus, this verse presents the psychological hallmark of liberation while living जीवन-मुक्ति (jīvanmukti): perfect poise in all circumstances, born of unshakable Self-knowledge.

—: Key Sanskrit Terms :—

Let us follow the subtle fragrance of wisdom, rising from the verse's pivotal Sanskrit terms, each carrying echoes of timeless truth, each like a flame that stands unwavering in windless air. Not elated, not dejected, steady in wisdom, they stand unmoved. Each syllable glows clear, undisturbed.

— ॐ —

न प्रहृष्येत् प्रियं प्राप्य (Na prahṛṣyet priyaṁ prāpya):

The Knower of Braham ब्रह्मविद् (brahmavid) does not प्रहृष्येत् prahṛṣyet — does not swell with delight — upon obtaining what is प्रियं priyam (pleasant).

Pleasure, though agreeable to the senses, is seen by him as a passing wave, incapable of touching the still ocean of his inner being.

— ॐ —

नोद्विजेत् प्राप्य च अप्रियम् (Nodvijet prāpya ca apriyam):

Nor does he उद्विजेत् udvijet — feel agitation or distress — when encountering अप्रियम् apriyam (unpleasant experiences).

Pain is met with the same equipoise as pleasure, for both are understood to be fleeting modes of प्रकृति prakṛti.

— ॐ —

स्थिरबुद्धिः (Sthirabuddhiḥ):

His intellect बुद्धि (buddhi) is स्थिर sthira — firm, steady, unmoved by the dualities of life.

Such steadiness is not born of repression but from a luminous perception of the imperishable Self beneath all changing conditions.

— ॐ —

असम्मूढः (Asammūḍhaḥ):

He is असम्मूढः asammūḍhaḥ — free from confusion, delusion, or bewilderment.

No longer mistaking the body, mind, or emotions as the Self, he abides in clarity, unwavering and pure.

— ॐ —

ब्रह्मविद् ब्रह्मणि स्थितः (Brahmavid brahmaṇi sthitaḥ):

The ब्रह्मविद् brahmavid — the knower of Braham — is स्थितः sthitah — firmly established — ब्रह्मणि brahmaṇi, in the very Reality he has realized.

Knowledge is not mere intellectual understanding, but a living, abiding identification with the Infinite.

Each word of the verse gently illumines for us the inner stature of the liberated sage: untouched by pleasure and pain, steady in wisdom, radiant in peace.

—: *In Brief* :—

— ॐ श्रीकृष्णाय नमः ॐ —

Here, Shri Krishna describes the supreme state of one who has realized Braham—"ब्रह्मविद् brahmavit"—not merely as an abstract concept, but as one's own innermost Self.

Such a person, "ब्रह्मणि स्थितः brahmaṇi sthitaḥ", is established in Braham—not only in moments of meditation, but at all times, in all states—waking, dreaming, or deep sleep.

The verse highlights a crucial spiritual quality: "न प्रहृष्येत्प्रियं प्राप्य नोद्विजेत्प्राप्य चाप्रियम् na prahṛṣyet priyaṁ prāpya, nodvijet prāpya cāpriyam"—he rejoices not upon encountering what is pleasant, nor is he distressed when faced with what is unpleasant. Why?

Because his inner identification with the eternal Self renders all transient conditions powerless to sway his consciousness. He sees both pleasant and unpleasant as mere modifications of prakṛti, born of past karmas, dancing upon the surface of the mind.

Such a sage no longer sees reality through the lens of likes and dislikes, gain and loss, joy and sorrow. His vision, purified by Self-knowledge, no longer reacts from egoic attachment.

He lives in the world but is not of it—he sees its fluctuations as one might watch waves rise and fall on the surface of the ocean, knowing that the beneath Depth, remains undisturbed.

— ॐ श्रीरामाय नमः ॐ —

The word "असम्मूढः asammūḍhaḥ" is significant—it refers to one whose understanding is completely free from delusion, unclouded by ignorance, and firm in discrimination (viveka).

He does not waver in judgment nor is his peace disrupted by the flux of circumstances.

This clarity is not the product of mere reasoning but the fruit of direct, intuitive knowledge of Braham—अपरोक्ष -अनुभूति aparokṣānubhūti.

— ॐ अधर्मनाशकाय नमः ॐ —

The true ब्रह्मविद् brahmavit is not merely a scholar or philosopher, but one who has merged the mind, intellect, and ego into the Absolute, leaving no trace of separateness.

He knows not only Braham as the substratum of all that exists, but also the illusoriness of individuality and the false reality of the world's dualities.

To such a one, the pleasant and unpleasant are but ephemeral waves, while Braham is the unchanging ocean.

— ॐ अनन्तगुण गम्भीराय नमः ॐ —

This verse also clarifies a subtle point: even sattva guṇa, though luminous and pure, is ultimately a limitation. For it still contains within it a subtle joy, a refined attachment to knowledge and virtue.

But the ब्रह्मविद् brahmavit, having transcended all three guṇas, does not even cling to the joy of sattva. Hence, he is truly गुणातीत guṇātīta, beyond the modes, and therefore unperturbed in all experiences.

Having described the sama-darśī—the one of equal vision—in the previous verses, here Shri Krishna portrays the interior equanimity of that sage. What he sees in all beings outwardly, he experiences within: the changeless peace of Braham.

In the verses that follow, Shri Krishna continues to elaborate the fruits of this realization—the inner freedom, peace, and joy of one who, having abandoned all egoic striving, lives immersed in the bliss of the Supreme.

— ॐ तत सत ॐ —

Before we move on, let us bow in reverence to this sacred verse. Write it by hand, reflect on its meaning, chant it aloud, make it your own.

— ॐ —

न प्रहृष्येत्प्रियं प्राप्य नोद्विजेत्प्राप्य चाप्रियम् ।
na prahṛṣyetpriyaṁ prāpya nodvijetprāpya cāpriyam
स्थिरबुद्धिरसम्मूढो ब्रह्मविद् ब्रह्मणि स्थितः ॥५-२०॥
sthirabuddhirasammūḍho brahmavid brahmaṇi sthitaḥ (5-20)

— ॐ —

न प्रहृष्येत्प्रियं प्राप्य नोद्विजेत्प्राप्य चाप्रियम् ।
na prahṛṣyetpriyaṁ prāpya nodvijetprāpya cāpriyam
स्थिरबुद्धिरसम्मूढो ब्रह्मविद् ब्रह्मणि स्थितः ॥५-२०॥
sthirabuddhirasammūḍho brahmavid brahmaṇi sthitaḥ (5-20)

ॐ तत्सदिति श्रीमद्भगवद्गीतासूपनिषत्सु ब्रह्मविद्यायां योगशास्त्रे श्रीकृष्णार्जुनसंवादे
om tatsaditi śrīmadbhagavadgītāsūpaniṣatsu brahmavidyāyāṁ yogaśāstre śrīkṛṣṇārjunasaṁvāde
संन्यासयोगो नाम पञ्चमोऽध्यायः श्लोकः २०
saṁnyāsayogo nāma pañcamo'dhyāyaḥ ślokaḥ 20

Om-Tat-Sat—Om (Braham) is the sole Reality. In the Yogic Scripture on the Science-of-Braham, the Shrimada-Bhāgvada-Gītā Upanishad, we hereby conclude Shloka 20 of the Dialogue between Shrī Krishna and Arjuna entitled Sanyāsa-Yoga, Canto V.

— ॐ श्रीसीतारमाभ्याम् नमः ॐ —

Be the Deep That Knows No Wave;
Not elated upon obtaining the sweet,
nor perturbed upon begetting the bitter.

O heart, become the Ocean vast and still—
Whose Depth stays calm—though tempests may lash at the beach.

Above and around, the world will toss in joy/grief,
Yet inward lies that silence which none can shake—let alone reach.
For the sage abides in Him, Krishna—the deathless tide—
Unswayed by pleasure, pain, ego, pride.

—o—

No praise can lift, no blame can weigh—
The Yogi walks on a Path that's beyond age, death, decay.

No draught of pride from triumph's cup he sips,
Nor weeps when losses swallow up—all his wins.
For him, all this was just a rolling reel,
Streaming shadowy-sparks o'er the one Reality: Braham.

—o—

The Yogi is first and foremost a ब्रह्मविद् brahmavid—
knower of Him who pervades 'neath form and name.
Knowing of Him, he dwells in Him,
Thus he abides ब्रह्मणि स्थितः Brahmaṇi sthitaḥ.

The yogi has folded himself into the eternal Infinite,
What need now,
To prove? To chase? To flee?

Neither shaken, nor stirred,
असम्मूढः Asammūḍhaḥ—undeluded he stays.
For he has seen the full trick:
The wheel, the play, the stage—above all: the Big Magician.

ॐ गीता श्लोकः ५.२१ – GĪTĀ VERSE 5.21

ॐ श्रीमद्भगवद्गीतासूपनिषत्सु ब्रह्मविद्यायां योगशास्त्रे श्रीकृष्णार्जुनसंवादे
om śrīmadbhagavadgītāsūpaniṣatsu brahmavidyāyāṁ yogaśāstre śrīkṛṣṇārjunasaṁvāde
संन्यासयोगो नाम पञ्चमोऽध्यायः श्लोकः २१
saṁnyāsayogo nāma pañcamo'dhyāyaḥ ślokaḥ 21

— ॐ —

बाह्यस्पर्शेष्वसक्तात्मा विन्दत्यात्मनि यत्सुखम् ।
bāhyasparśeṣvasaktātmā vindatyātmani yatsukham
स ब्रह्मयोगयुक्तात्मा सुखमक्षयमश्नुते ॥५-२१॥
sa brahmayogayuktātmā sukhamakṣayamaśnute (5-21)

One whose mind remains unattached to the external objects of senses, attains to the inner Sāttvika joy which is inherent in the Self. Such a Yogī—with his mind completely identified with Brahama, through absorption in it—forever enjoys undecaying bliss. (5.21)

—: *Word-by-Word* :—

बाह्यस्पर्शेषु bāhya-sparśeṣu – in external contacts; असक्तात्मा asakta-ātmā – with a detached mind; विन्दति vindati – finds; आत्मनि ātmani – within the self; यत् yat – which; सुखम् sukham – happiness; सः saḥ – he; ब्रह्मयोगयुक्तात्मा brahma-yoga-yukta-ātmā – one united with Braham in yoga; सुखम् sukham – bliss; अक्षयम् akṣayam – imperishable; अश्नुते aśnute – attains.

—: *Understanding The Verse* :—

— ॐ श्रीकृष्णाय नमः ॐ —

In this verse, Bhagwāna Shri Krishna reveals the inner bliss of the Yogī—one who has withdrawn from the seductive pull of external sense objects and turned inward in pursuit of the Self.

Unlike the fleeting joys that arise from contact with the outer world, the joy here is of a higher order: it is Sāttvika, serene and luminous, springing not from objects but from nearness to the very nature of the Self.

— ॐ श्रीरामाय नमः ॐ —

The verse declares that the yogi—whose mind is unattached to external sensory contacts and has discovered the joy that dwells within—finds lasting fulfillment: not in worldly achievements, but in the still and radiant presence of Braham, the Supreme Reality.

Such a one abides in eternal bliss, for his mind is wholly absorbed and identified within satt-chitt-ānanda braham, the ocean of existence-bliss-consciousness.

This verse, therefore, marks a turning inward—a recognition that true and abiding happiness arises not from changeable conditions, but from Self-realization through inner absorption and detachment.

—: Key Sanskrit Terms :—

Let us attune to the silent music of the verse and see how its key Sanskrit expressions compose a symphony of concealed meanings. Let us rest with the Sanskrit as with cool shade at noon. Detached from outer contact, rejoicing in Self, one finds the inexhaustible nectar. Each word soothes with inward sweetness.

— ॐ —

बाह्यस्पर्शेषु असक्तात्मा (Bāhyasparśeṣu asaktātmā):

The असक्तात्मा asaktātmā — one whose soul is free of attachment — does not cling to बाह्य-स्पर्श bāhya-sparśa — the external contacts of the senses with their objects.

Sensual pleasures, being external and fleeting, no longer hold sway over his inner peace.

— ॐ —

विन्दति आत्मनि यत् सुखम् (Vindaty ātmani yat sukham):

He विन्दति vindati — finds, discovers —यत् सुखम् yat sukham — that deep, inner joy — आत्मनि ātmani — in the Self itself.

This bliss is not dependent on objects or circumstances, but wells up naturally from the realization of the Self's luminous, immortal nature.

— ॐ —

सः ब्रह्मयोगयुक्तात्मा (Saḥ brahmayogayuktātmā):

Such a one is ब्रह्मयोगयुक्तात्मा brahma-yoga-yuktātmā — whose soul is fully yoked, merged, and absorbed in Braham through the Yoga of Knowledge.

His consciousness is united with the Infinite, no longer fragmented by desires.

— ॐ —

सुखम् अक्षयम् अश्नुते (Sukham akṣayam aśnute):

He अश्नुते aśnute — enjoys — अक्षय सुखम् akṣayam sukham — the undecaying, inexhaustible bliss that is not subject to the ravages of time, not dependent on the flux of the external world, but eternal, boundless, self-existent.

This beautiful verse so well portrays the journey inward: from the restless pursuit of outer pleasures to the serene discovery of the everlasting within joy.

—: In Brief :—

— ॐ श्रीकृष्णाय नमः ॐ —

In this sacred teaching, Shri Krishna describes the inner victory of the one who, having turned away from outer allurements, finds in the Self the wellspring of joy.

The phrase "बाह्यस्पर्शेष्वसक्तात्मा bāhyasparśeṣv asaktātmā" refers to one whose ātmā, or mind and heart, is no longer entangled in the sensory objects of the external world—sound, touch, form, taste, and smell.

— ॐ श्रीरामाय नमः ॐ —

These sense-contacts स्पर्शाः (sparśāḥ) may temporarily please, but they are inherently unstable and ultimately unsatisfying.

They are dependent on external circumstances, which are themselves impermanent. The wise Yogi understands this and withdraws, not out of aversion or repression, but out of a higher longing—a yearning for the unchanging, self-existent bliss that is not subject to the fluctuations of gain and loss, pleasure and pain.

— ॐ दशरथात्मजाय नमः ॐ —

The joy that arises in the interiority of Self-contemplation is called सात्त्विक सुख Sāttvika sukha—a joy pure, luminous, and subtle.

It is described here as "आत्मनि यत् सुखम् ātmani yat sukham"—the bliss that is found in the Self. This is not pleasure born of stimulation, but peace born of absorption within Braham. It is the quiet ecstasy known only to the one who has merged the mind in Braham.

— ॐ आर्याय नमः ॐ —

"स ब्रह्मयोगयुक्तात्मा Sa brahma-yoga-yuktātmā"—such a person is said to be united with Braham through Yoga. His inner instrument अन्तः करण (antaḥkaraṇa) has been purified, and through deep meditation ध्यान (dhyāna), he has merged the ego and intellect into Braham-consciousness.

Thusly, he enjoys "अक्षयम् सुखम् akṣayam sukham"—an imperishable bliss, not dependent on time, space, or causality.

In the next verse, Shri Krishna will continue by explaining why the wise reject external pleasures: because they are sources of sorrow, born of contact, and bound to end.

This way Bhagwāna Shri Krishna is preparing us to recognize the illusory promise of external pleasure and turn within, toward the indwelling Supreme.

— ॐ तत सत ॐ —

Before we move on, let us bow in reverence to this sacred verse. Write it by hand, reflect on its meaning, chant it aloud, make it your own.

— ॐ —

बाह्यस्पर्शेष्वसक्तात्मा विन्दत्यात्मनि यत्सुखम् ।
bāhyasparśeṣvasaktātmā vindatyātmani yatsukham
स ब्रह्मयोगयुक्तात्मा सुखमक्षयमश्नुते ॥५-२१॥
sa brahmayogayuktātmā sukhamakṣayamaśnute (5-21)

—ॐ—

बाह्यस्पर्शेष्वसक्तात्मा विन्दत्यात्मनि यत्सुखम् ।
bāhyasparśeṣvasaktātmā vindatyātmani yatsukham
स ब्रह्मयोगयुक्तात्मा सुखमक्षयमश्नुते ॥५-२१॥
sa brahmayogayuktātmā sukhamakṣayamaśnute (5-21)

ॐ तत्सदिति श्रीमद्भगवद्गीतासूपनिषत्सु ब्रह्मविद्यायां योगशास्त्रे श्रीकृष्णार्जुनसंवादे
om tatsaditi śrīmadbhagavadgītāsūpaniṣatsu brahmavidyāyāṁ yogaśāstre śrīkṛṣṇārjunasaṁvāde
संन्यासयोगो नाम पञ्चमोऽध्यायः श्लोकः २१
saṁnyāsayogo nāma pañcamo'dhyāyaḥ ślokaḥ 21

Om-Tat-Sat—Om (Braham) is the sole Reality. In the Yogic Scripture on the Science-of-Braham, the Shrimada-Bhāgvada-Gītā Upanishad, we hereby conclude Shloka 21 of the Dialogue between Shrī Krishna and Arjuna entitled Sanyāsa-Yoga, Canto V.

— ॐ योगिनां पतये नमः ॐ —

Gita's words here are like the wind from before Time.
They speak of world-conquest—not by sword, but by sameness.
This is not sameness of form—but of vision.
Know O mortal: the seer who sees without tremble, without tilt,
has already conquered half the world.

— o —

The wise does not flee from sorrow or joy.
It has come unbidden; and so unmoved there he stands, watching
—witnessing how it will move past.
He sees the world not as cruel or kind—
but simply as a show of waves passing by.

ॐ गीता श्लोकः ५.२२ – Gītā Verse 5.22

ॐ श्रीमद्भगवद्गीतासूपनिषत्सु ब्रह्मविद्यायां योगशास्त्रे श्रीकृष्णार्जुनसंवादे
om śrīmadbhagavadgītāsūpaniṣatsu brahmavidyāyāṁ yogaśāstre śrīkṛṣṇārjunasaṁvāde
संन्यासयोगो नाम पञ्चमोऽध्यायः श्लोकः २२
saṁnyāsayogo nāma pañcamo'dhyāyaḥ ślokaḥ 22

— ॐ —

ये हि संस्पर्शजा भोगा दुःखयोनय एव ते ।
ye hi saṁsparśajā bhogā duḥkhayonaya eva te
आद्यन्तवन्तः कौन्तेय न तेषु रमते बुधः ॥५-२२॥
ādyantavantaḥ kaunteya na teṣu ramate budhaḥ (5-22)

Pleasures born of sense-contacts are the very founts of miseries, O Kuntī-son; they have a beginning and an end, and the wise never really rejoices in such ephemeral delights. (5.22)

—: *Word-by-Word* :—

ये ye – those; हि hi – indeed; संस्पर्शजाः saṁsparśajāḥ – born of contact with the senses; भोगाः bhogāḥ – pleasures; दुःखयोनयः duḥkha-yonayaḥ – sources of misery; एव eva – only; ते te – they are; आद्यन्तवन्तः ādyantavantaḥ – having a beginning and an end; कौन्तेय kaunteya – O son of Kunti (Arjuna); न na – not; तेषु teṣu – in them; रमते ramate – delights; बुधः budhaḥ – the wise.

—: *Understanding The Verse* :—

— ॐ श्रीकृष्णाय नमः ॐ —

In this verse, Bhagwāna Shri Krishna directly warns against the deceptive nature of pleasures that arise from sense-contact.

These physical pleasures—विषय-आनन्द viṣay-ānanda—though appearing alluring and joyful, are in truth the very seeds of sorrow.

They are born of contact between the senses and their objects, and as such, are bound by time—they have a beginning and an end.

— ॐ ब्रह्मचारिणे नमः ॐ —

The wise, says the Lord, do not rejoice in such pleasures, knowing them to be ephemeral and binding.

Their fleeting nature causes craving and aversion, which lead to agitation, disappointment, and ultimately suffering.

This verse continues the teaching that true bliss lies not in the outer world, but in turning inward, toward the Self—Braham, the unchanging source of real and lasting joy.

By addressing Arjuna as Kaunteya, son of Kuntī, the Lord subtly reminds him of his noble lineage, born of a mother renowned for her austerity and detachment, thereby invoking the higher संस्कार samskāras latent within him.

—: Key Sanskrit Terms :—

We shall open the door of this verse through its Sanskrit syllables, and with each word, step deeper into the stillness of the inner light—each word showcasing worldly fruits that are already starting to rot even as they tempt. Each syllable a truth unembellished which warns softly: the joys born of sense-contact are wombs of sorrow, with beginning and end.

— ॐ —

ये हि संस्पर्शजा भोगाः (Ye hi saṁsparśajā bhogāḥ):

The pleasures भोगाः (bhogāḥ) that arise from संस्पर्श saṁsparśa — the contact between senses and sense-objects — are here described.

Such pleasures are not born of the Self, but are जा jā — generated — externally, fragile and dependent, and therefore ultimately unreliable.

— ॐ —

दुःखयोनयः एव ते (Duḥkhayonayaḥ eva te):

These pleasures are दुःख-योनयः duḥkha-yonayaḥ — veritable wombs of sorrow.

What begins as enjoyment sows the seeds of suffering — through attachment, longing, loss, and the inevitable dissatisfaction that follows.

— ॐ —

आद्यन्तवन्तः (Ādyantavantaḥ):

They are आदि-अंत-वन्तः ādi-anta-vantaḥ — possessing a beginning and an end.

All that has a beginning in time is destined to perish.

Thus, sense pleasures are impermanent, and their fleeting nature carries within itself the sorrow of upcoming loss.

— ॐ —

न तेषु रमते बुधः (Na teṣu ramate budhaḥ):

The बुधः budhaḥ — the awakened, the wise one — does न रमते na ramate — does not delight — in such pleasures.

Knowing their essential nature as ephemeral and binding, the sage turns his heart away, seeking only the undying bliss within.

The verse quietly unfolds the nature of worldly enjoyment, and of the serene wisdom which renounces it in favor of the Eternal.

—: In Brief :—

— ॐ श्रीकृष्णाय नमः ॐ —

Shri Krishna speaks here with directness and compassion: "ये हि संस्पर्शजा भोगा दुःखयोनय एव ते ye hi saṁsparśajā bhogā duḥkha-yonaya eva te"—the enjoyments that are born of sense-contact are indeed the wombs of sorrow.

Though they may appear as joy in the moment, their nature is deceptive.

Just as the flame attracts the moth only to consume it, so too do the fleeting pleasures of the world entice the unwise—only to deliver them to grief.

— ॐ श्रीरामाय नमः ॐ —

The phrase दुःखयोनय duḥkha-yonayaḥ—literally "wombs of suffering"—is quite startling. It does not merely say that these pleasures can lead to sorrow, but that they are inherently constituted as the very source of suffering—like the wake that ensues behind motion.

Even in their rise, they bring attachment, fear of loss, craving for repetition—and when they pass, they leave behind emptiness, restlessness, and despair.

That they have a beginning and an end आदि अंत वन्तः (ādy-antavantaḥ) is further proof of their unreality.

The wise बुधः (buddhāḥ), who have discerned the impermanent and perishable nature of all sense-bound experience, do not rejoice in them.

The happiness of the intelligent is rooted in that which is unchanging, self-luminous, and eternal—ब्रह्म Braham.

— ॐ अच्युताय नमः ॐ —

The deluded mind, steeped in ignorance अविद्या (avidyā), perceives external pleasures as true joy. But this is मिथ्य-आनन्द mithyā-ānanda, false delight—and it is not to be confused with the आनन्द ānanda of the Self, which is self-existent and independent of all contacts.

The ignorant chase after pleasure, not realizing that each indulgence sows seeds for future dissatisfaction and bondage.

— ॐ कंसारयाय नमः ॐ —

Sense pleasures not only bind the soul to संसार saṁsāra (the cycle of birth and death), but also agitate the mind, weaken the senses, and lead to further desires. Once entangled, the being becomes prey to काम-क्रोध-लोभ kāma, krodha, lobha—lust, anger, and greed—which drag the soul deeper into the mire of karma.

To drive this truth home, Shri Krishna addresses Arjuna as कौन्तेय Kaunteya, evoking the spiritual austerity and inner strength of his mother कुन्ती Kuntī.

Kuntī's own life was marked by dispassion and devotion, and Krishna subtly calls Arjuna to awaken that same virtue within himself: to rise above transient pleasures and seek the imperishable joy of Self-realization.

— ॐ परमात्मने नमः ॐ —

The wise avoid sense-born pleasures through deep discrimination —not out of repression, but out of love for tranquility.

Having known the eternal bliss of Braham, they have no interest in shadows. They do not need to renounce the world—they simply see through it.

This verse is often a turning point in people's life—shifting the seeker's attention away from the external, and pointing it inwards.

In the next verse, Bhagwāna Shri Krishna will extol the greatness of the one who has mastered desire itself—the conqueror of lust, who finds lasting peace even before leaving the body.

— ॐ तत सत ॐ —

Before moving on, let us once more bow in deep reverence before this sacred verse of the Bhagavad-Gītā, an eternal beacon of wisdom that ceaselessly illumines the path of seekers. Engage with its form—inscribe it with your own hand, let your heart dwell upon its meaning, and raise your voice in its chanting—for within these syllables echoes the undying proclamation delivered millennia ago on the battlefield of Kurukshetra. These words, transmitted unchanged across the unbroken chain of generations, form a living bridge, linking us to that sanctified era when Bhagwāna Shri Krishna Himself walked this earth and bestowed this divine teaching. Through the luminous vibration of these sacred Sanskrit sounds, we are drawn nearer to His timeless presence, touching the very heartbeat of the Eternal.

— ॐ —

ये हि संस्पर्शजा भोगा दुःखयोनय एव ते ।
ye hi saṁsparśajā bhogā duḥkhayonaya eva te
आद्यन्तवन्तः कौन्तेय न तेषु रमते बुधः ॥५-२२॥
ādyantavantaḥ kaunteya na teṣu ramate budhaḥ (5-22)

— ॐ —
ये हि संस्पर्शजा भोगा दुःखयोनय एव ते ।
ye hi saṁsparśajā bhogā duḥkhayonaya eva te
आद्यन्तवन्तः कौन्तेय न तेषु रमते बुधः ॥५-२२॥
ādyantavantaḥ kaunteya na teṣu ramate budhaḥ (5-22)

ॐ तत्सदिति श्रीमद्भगवद्गीतासूपनिषत्सु ब्रह्मविद्यायां योगशास्त्रे श्रीकृष्णार्जुनसंवादे
om tatsaditi śrīmadbhagavadgītāsūpaniṣatsu brahmavidyāyāṁ yogaśāstre śrīkṛṣṇārjunasaṁvāde
संन्यासयोगो नाम पञ्चमोऽध्यायः श्लोकः २२
saṁnyāsayogo nāma pañcamo'dhyāyaḥ ślokaḥ 22

Om-Tat-Sat—Om (Braham) is the sole Reality. In the Yogic Scripture on the Science-of-Braham, the Shrimada-Bhāgvada-Gītā Upanishad, we hereby conclude Shloka 22 of the Dialogue between Shrī Krishna and Arjuna entitled Sanyāsa-Yoga, Canto V.

— ॐ परमानन्दाय नमः ॐ —

Caught Up in this Passing Dream?

O seeker, wake to the inner Sāttvika joy of the Self!
This world of dust is but a dream: a fleeting gust.
The Yogi looks at these shifting tides,
But he remains unmoved—staying abided in Bliss.

A thousand years, one life, a million, a breath, a sigh,
What difference? It matters not—Time doth keep passing by.
For the Yogi whose mind is free and identified with Braham,
He holds all within himself—within the eternity of his own Self.

In Oneness with satt-chitt-ananda braham!

Ah! What's this state, this bliss untold,
Beyond form/name—which neither thought nor word can hold!

No knower here, nor known doth be,
No other here. No this-that. No difference. No Unity.
Beyond the Waking, Dream, and Deep,
A silence vastness—a thoughtless Sleep.
No Third, no Fourth, no earth-space-air—
i am the boundless Bliss of Braham—beyond compare.

ॐ गीता श्लोकः ५.२३ – GĪTĀ VERSE 5.23

ॐ श्रीमद्भगवद्गीतासूपनिषत्सु ब्रह्मविद्यायां योगशास्त्रे श्रीकृष्णार्जुनसंवादे
om śrīmadbhagavadgītāsūpaniṣatsu brahmavidyāyāṁ yogaśāstre śrīkṛṣṇārjunasaṁvāde
संन्यासयोगो नाम पञ्चमोऽध्यायः श्लोकः २३
saṁnyāsayogo nāma pañcamo'dhyāyaḥ ślokaḥ 23

— ॐ —

शक्नोतीहैव यः सोढुं प्राक्शरीरविमोक्षणात् ।
śaknotīhaiva yaḥ soḍhuṁ prākśarīravimokṣaṇāt
कामक्रोधोद्भवं वेगं स युक्तः स सुखी नरः ॥५-२३॥
kāmakrodhodbhavaṁ vegaṁ sa yuktaḥ sa sukhī naraḥ (5-23)

He who is able to withstand the urges of lust and anger in this very life, before the body drops off, he alone is said to be poised, he alone poised for everlasting happiness. (5.23)

—: Word-by-Word :—

शक्नोति śaknoti – is able; इह एव iha eva – here itself; यः yaḥ – who; सोढुम् soḍhum – to withstand; प्राक् prāk – before; शरीरविमोक्षणात् śarīra-vimokṣaṇāt – liberation from the body; कामक्रोधोद्भवम् kāma-krodha-udbhavam – arising from desire and anger; वेगम् vegam – the impulse; सः saḥ – he; युक्तः yuktaḥ – is disciplined; सः saḥ – he; सुखी sukhī – is happy; नरः naraḥ – man.

—: Understanding The Verse :—

— ॐ श्रीकृष्णाय नमः ॐ —

In this verse, Bhagwāna Shri Krishna declares the essential qualification for lasting happiness: mastery over the impulses of desire काम (kāma) and anger क्रोध (krodha) while still living in the body.

The Lord does not speak of passive avoidance or repression, but of a conscious and steadfast ability to withstand these inner storms.

— ॐ श्रीरामाय नमः ॐ —

The verse emphasizes the urgency and difficulty of this task—these urges must be conquered before the fall of the body (i.e., during embodied life). Thus, spiritual growth is not to be postponed for some later existence, nor is it complete with theoretical knowledge alone.

Conquest over lust and anger is the necessary gateway to enduring joy—the joy that is not born of contact or circumstance, but which arises from Self-mastery and inner peace.

This teaching affirms that spiritual practice is not merely intellectual or ceremonial—it demands psychological purification and the unwavering discipline of the mind.

—: Key Sanskrit Terms :—

Let us gaze into the mirror of this verse, where its Sanskrit words shimmer with layered beauty and secret depth. Each of these words is a weapon of dispassion held in our still hands. "He who endures impulse before death, freed of desire and anger, is a yogi, happy." Each word here is discipline ripened into serenity.

— ॐ —

शक्नोति इह एव यः सोढुं (Śaknoti ihaiva yaḥ soḍhum):

Here, शक्नोति śaknoti — "he who is able" — indicates true inner strength, not physical might but the power of self-mastery.

इह एव Ihaiva — "here itself," in this embodied existence — signifies the urgency: while living, in this very world, not after death.

— ॐ —

प्राक् शरीर विमोक्षणात् (Prāk śarīra vimokṣaṇāt):

प्राक् Prāk — "before" — शरीर विमोक्षणात् śarīravimokṣaṇāt — "the release of the body," or physical death.

Liberation must be won before the body's fall; it is to be achieved now, not deferred to some future state.

— ॐ —

कामक्रोधोद्भवं वेगं (Kāmakrodhodbhavaṁ vegaṁ):

The वेग vega — intense surge or impulse — arising from काम kāma (desire) and क्रोध krodha (anger) is a mighty force that sweeps away the unwary.

These twin passions are the primal disturbances of the soul, the great enemies of peace.

— ॐ —

स युक्तः (Sa yuktaḥ):

He who withstands these inner storms is युक्तः yuktaḥ — firmly yoked to Yoga, established in self-mastery and equanimity.

— ॐ —

स सुखी नरः (Sa sukhī naraḥ):

He is the सुखी नरः sukhī naraḥ — the truly happy man.

Not in fleeting pleasures, but in the conquest of inner turmoil lies the doorway to lasting, undecaying happiness.

This lovely verse reveals the nature of true spiritual strength: the mastery over inner forces, here and now—and which alone leads to unshakeable abiding bliss.

—: In Brief :—

— ॐ श्रीकृष्णाय नमः ॐ —

Shri Krishna says: "**शक्नोतीहैव यः सोढुं** ... śaknotīhaiva yaḥ soḍhuṁ... "—he who can endure, in this very life, the powerful surges of desire and anger, is truly poised **युक्तः** (yuktaḥ), and is alone truly happy **सुखी नरः** (sukhī naraḥ).

This is a profound call to vigilance and inner heroism.

The words **काम-क्रोध** kāma and krodha represent not only individual impulses but also the two most powerful enemies of the soul, born of delusion and ignorance.

Desire arises when the mind projects happiness upon external objects; anger follows when those desires are obstructed. Both spring from the same root—misidentification with the body-mind complex and its attachments.

These urges are not easily subdued. They do not vanish with one act of will or an isolated moment of insight. Rather, they arise again and again, fed by memory, habit, sense-contact, and imagination.

Therefore, Shri Krishna uses the word "**वेगं** vega"—meaning surge, force, or current—to indicate their violent, sweeping nature. Like floods, they can overwhelm the unprepared aspirant.

— ॐ श्रीरामाय नमः ॐ —

The true yogī is not one who simply performs outer austerities or renunciations, but one who, through steady discrimination **विवेक** (viveka), renunciation **वैराग्य** (vairāgya), and meditation **ध्यान** (dhyāna), becomes inwardly firm—able to stand like a mountain amidst the storm, allowing these impulses to rise and fall without being moved.

— ॐ विश्वात्मने नमः ॐ —

It is also important that the Lord adds: "**इह एव** iha eva"—here and now, in this very life.

The conquest of passion and anger is not postponed to some celestial realm or posthumous liberation. It must occur in the embodied condition, while the soul still struggles through the path of effort.

To squander human life in indulgence or heedlessness is, as the tradition says, a great loss, for the human birth is rare, and even rarer is the opportunity for liberation.

— ॐ ताटकान्तकाय नमः ॐ —

Moreover, the verse implies that this victory over inner enemies is the prerequisite for lasting happiness. The worldly man pursues happiness through gratification of desire, but the yogī attains it through freedom from desire itself.

The wise have realized that no object, no relationship, no pleasure of the senses can yield abiding peace, because all are transient and laced with expectation and fear.

The one who has subdued lust and anger is not dependent upon anything outside himself—and is therefore **सुखी** sukhī, truly blessed.

— ॐ वालिप्रतापहन्त्रे नमः ॐ —

The word **नरः** naraḥ here, as tradition holds, signifies not merely a man in the biological sense, but a noble soul—one who has risen above the animalistic tendencies of craving, aggression, and ego.

— **ॐ वेदविद्याविशारदाय नमः ॐ** —Such a being is a true human, a realized one, who reflects the divine potential latent in all.

— ॐ वानरसेनासंवृताय नमः ॐ —

This verse stands as a spiritual measure: Who is fit for Yoga? Who is ripe for peace? It is not he who merely talks of truth, but he who has vanquished the foes within—the fires of desire and the poison of anger. In such a one, the light of Braham shines steadily.

With this, Shri Krishna completes a key progression—from sense-restraint, to the joy of inner meditation, to the fearless freedom of the self-controlled sage.

The next verses will further describe the **ब्रह्मभूतः** brahmabhūtaḥ—the one who has become Braham by living in that light of realization.

— ॐ तत सत ॐ —

Before we move on, let us bow in reverence to this sacred verse—a timeless beacon of wisdom guiding seekers for ages. Write it by hand, reflect on its meaning, and chant it aloud, for these sounds alone carry the authenticity of that era. The world may have changed but the living vibration of these Sanskrit sounds still remain as original as they were when Bhagwān Shri Krishna Himself walked the earth and imparted these teachings.

— ॐ —

शक्नोतीहैव यः सोढुं प्राक्शरीरविमोक्षणात् ।
śaknotīhaiva yaḥ soḍhuṁ prākśarīravimokṣaṇāt
कामक्रोधोद्भवं वेगं स युक्तः स सुखी नरः ॥५-२३॥
kāmakrodhodbhavaṁ vegaṁ sa yuktaḥ sa sukhī naraḥ (5-23)

—ॐ—

शक्नोतीहैव यः सोढुं प्राक्शरीरविमोक्षणात् ।
śaknotīhaiva yaḥ soḍhuṁ prākśarīravimokṣaṇāt
कामक्रोधोद्भवं वेगं स युक्तः स सुखी नरः ॥५-२३॥
kāmakrodhodbhavaṁ vegaṁ sa yuktaḥ sa sukhī naraḥ (5-23)

ॐ तत्सदिति श्रीमद्भगवद्गीतासूपनिषत्सु ब्रह्मविद्यायां योगशास्त्रे श्रीकृष्णार्जुनसंवादे
om tatsaditi śrīmadbhagavadgītāsūpaniṣatsu brahmavidyāyāṁ yogaśāstre śrīkṛṣṇārjunasaṁvāde
संन्यासयोगो नाम पञ्चमोऽध्यायः श्लोकः २३
saṁnyāsayogo nāma pañcamo'dhyāyaḥ ślokaḥ 23

Om-Tat-Sat—Om (Braham) is the sole Reality. In the Yogic Scripture on the Science-of-Braham, the Shrimada-Bhāgvada-Gītā Upanishad, we hereby conclude Shloka 23 of the Dialogue between Shrī Krishna and Arjuna entitled Sanyāsa-Yoga, Canto V.

— ॐ रामलक्ष्मणभरतशत्रुघ्नात्मने नमः ॐ —

. The "Gateway-to-Bliss" Stands Sealed with a Flame
In the dusky womb of mortal clay, an unseen fire stays lit,
Where, midst heavy colored apparitions,
The twin-dragons —Lust & Wrath— remaining entwined,
keep dancing unremittingly!

Now who shall still the serpent's cry?
Who shall bind the burning dragon's eye?
The dragons dance in mind's pale hall; they roar for fleeting taste—
And only he who withstands their fiery breath—
Shall enter the Gateway and have Death itself effaced!

Shri Krishna speaks in thunder-voice:
"Before the body's fall,
Stand firm and conquer passion's tide and flame—
Heed now this timeless call, O mortal."

Fire and flood within the breast—
Man is tried and man is blessed.
But he who walks through anger / lust,
And casts them both into the dust—
He alone shall rise on wings of flame,
—Freed from sorrows—freed from treachery—freed from world—
And enter the Gateway to Untold Bliss.

ॐ गीता श्लोकः ५.२४ – GĪTĀ VERSE 5.24

ॐ श्रीमद्भगवद्गीतासूपनिषत्सु ब्रह्मविद्यायां योगशास्त्रे श्रीकृष्णार्जुनसंवादे
om śrīmadbhagavadgītāsūpaniṣatsu brahmavidyāyāṁ yogaśāstre śrīkṛṣṇārjunasaṁvāde
संन्यासयोगो नाम पञ्चमोऽध्यायः श्लोकः २४
saṁnyāsayogo nāma pañcamo'dhyāyaḥ ślokaḥ 24

— ॐ —

योऽन्तःसुखोऽन्तरारामस्तथान्तर्ज्योतिरेव यः ।
yo'ntaḥsukho'ntarārāmastathāntarjyotireva yaḥ
स योगी ब्रह्मनिर्वाणं ब्रह्मभूतोऽधिगच्छति ॥५-२४॥
sa yogī brahmanirvāṇaṁ brahmabhūto'dhigacchati (5-24)

He who is content within the Self, who partakes of the joy of the Self, who is illumined with the inner light—that Yogī fixed on Brahama, attains mergence in Brahama: who is all peace. (5.24)

—: *Word-by-Word* :—

यः yaḥ – who; अन्तःसुखः antaḥ-sukhaḥ – finds happiness within; अन्तरारामः antar-ārāmaḥ – rejoices within; तथा tathā – and; एव यः eva yaḥ – and whose; अन्तर्ज्योतिः antarjyoti – light is within; सः saḥ – that; योगी yogī – yogi; ब्रह्मनिर्वाणम् brahma-nirvāṇam – liberation in Braham; ब्रह्मभूतः brahma-bhūtaḥ – being one with Braham; अधिगच्छति adhigacchati – attains.

—: *Understanding The Verse* :—

— ॐ श्रीकृष्णाय नमः ॐ —

In this verse, Bhagwāna Shri Krishna describes the inner fulfillment and spiritual radiance of the true Yogī—one who is wholly established in the Self.

This is the sage who has turned inward, and who neither seeks pleasure in the outer world nor relies on sensory experiences for joy. Instead, he draws all satisfaction from the Self alone.

Such a one is described as rejoicing within, illumined from within, and content within the Self.

— ॐ श्रीरामाय नमः ॐ —

The verse highlights the threefold characteristics of the liberated sage: inner contentment, inner delight, and inner illumination. These are not metaphorical embellishments, but the natural outcome of deep and sustained realization.

This Yogī is ब्रह्मभूतः brahma-bhūtaḥ – of the nature of Braham;

He is ब्रह्म-युक्तात्मा brahma-yogayuktātmā—his mind stays yoked to Braham, the Supreme;

and the fruit of such perfect absorption is ब्रह्मनिर्वाणम Brahma-nirvāṇa—complete liberation and merger into Braham, who is the embodiment of peace, knowledge, and bliss.

—: Key Sanskrit Terms :—

Let us hold the Sanskrit terms like river stones, turning them over in the stream of the verse, watching how they glint, how they shift, how they settle into clarity.

— ॐ —

योऽन्तःसुखः (Yo'ntaḥsukhaḥ):

The one who delights in अन्तःसुखः antaḥsukha — inner joy — who finds his happiness not in external circumstances, but in the silent bliss of the Self (Ātmā).

This joy is independent, self-arising, needing no support from outer objects.

— ॐ —

अन्तरारामः (Antarārāmaḥ):

The one who आरामः ārāmaḥ — rejoices, rests — within himself. His heart is not scattered over fleeting pleasures, but anchored in the quiet garden of the Self.

The soul's repose is inward, serene, ever-renewing.

— ॐ —

अन्तर्ज्योतिः एव यः (Antarjyotiḥ eva yaḥ):

The one whose light ज्योतिः (jyotiḥ) shines from अन्तः within.

Such a soul is illumined not by the fire of senses, nor by external knowledge, but by the inner effulgence of pure awareness — the light of Braham itself.

— ॐ —

स योगी ब्रह्मनिर्वाणम् (Sa yogī brahmanirvāṇam):

Such a yogī — one steadfast in union — attains ब्रह्मनिर्वाण brahmanirvāṇa — the final dissolution into Braham, the perfect peace where all dualities cease, and the soul rests in its own infinite essence.

— ॐ —

ब्रह्मभूतः अधिगच्छति (Brahmabhūtaḥ adhigacchati):

Having become ब्रह्मभूतः brahmabhūtaḥ — of the nature of Braham — he does not merely "reach" Braham as an external goal; he becomes Braham, realizing his own Self as the Self of all.

This beautiful verse paints the luminous portrait of the liberated one — inwardly fulfilled, self-illumined, and absorbed in the Infinite. Each syllable glows with fullness as it shows the sage who is one with Braham—rejoicing in the inner light, content in the Self, radiant.

—: In Brief :—

— ॐ श्रीकृष्णाय नमः ॐ —

Shri Krishna here unfolds the inner majesty of the liberated Yogī, one who is "अन्तःसुखः अन्तरारामः अन्तर्ज्योतिः antaḥ-sukhaḥ, antaḥ-rāmaḥ, antaḥ-jyotiḥ"—happy within, delighting within, and illumined from within.

This is not a temporary withdrawal or a meditative exercise. It is the natural state of one who has realized the Self—not as an idea, but as the one eternal reality.

The pleasures of the senses no longer attract such a sage because he has discovered a joy that is uncaused, unshaken, and unending.

— ॐ श्रीरामाय नमः ॐ —

The term "अन्तःसुखः antaḥ-sukhaḥ" signifies that the sage no longer depends on external objects for happiness. His joy arises from the Self, which is complete, full, and ever-content.

This is not a joy born of experience, but of being—the quiet bliss of resting in one's true nature.

"अन्तरारामः Antaḥ-rāmaḥ" describes the inward-turning mind that finds its play and delight in Braham. Such a person no longer seeks stimulation in the world, for he has tasted the nectar of divine Selfhood. His joy is not passive or blank, but a celebration of the Infinite within.

— ॐ शूराय नमः ॐ —

"अन्तर्ज्योतिः Antaḥ-jyotiḥ" denotes one who is illumined not by the light of the sun, moon, or fire, but by the light of consciousness itself.

The light that shines in the heart of all beings—the light of the Ātmā—is fully awakened in him. He lives in that light, and sees by it.

Such a person is said to be "ब्रह्म -युक्तात्मा brahma-yoga-yuktātmā"—his mind yoked inseparably to Braham. This is not mere concentration, but total union. His thoughts, emotions, identity—all have been surrendered into the Absolute.

There is no trace of ego or separateness. Thus, he is no longer just a seeker—he is a knower, a realizer, a liberated being.

— ॐ आत्मरूपाय नमः ॐ —

The fruit of this state is "ब्रह्मनिर्वाणम् brahma-nirvāṇam"—a merger into Braham, the Supreme, who is शान्तः śāntaḥ—the essence of peace.

Here, निर्वाण nirvāṇa does not mean annihilation, but the extinction of ignorance, ego, and suffering, leaving only the pure awareness of the Absolute.

This liberation is not something attained after death. It is the living liberation (जीवन मुक्ति jīvanmukti) of one who is free while still embodied.

To such a one, the world may continue, but it has no binding power. He moves through it like the wind—untouched, serene, and radiant.

— ॐ पितृ भक्ताय नमः ॐ —

The verse subtly affirms that ब्रह्म Braham is not a distant concept to be worshipped as other—it is the very Self, to be known directly, lived intimately, and merged into with reverent love and unwavering knowledge.

Thus, Shri Krishna unfolds the glory of the योगी Yogī who has completed the journey inward. In the following verses, He will continue to elaborate on this state—describing the condition and characteristics of those who have attained ब्रह्मनिर्वाण brahma-nirvāṇa, and the supreme peace that surpasses all understanding.

— ॐ तत सत ॐ —

Before we move on, let us bow in reverence to this sacred verse. Write it by hand, reflect on its meaning, chant it aloud, make it your own.

— ॐ —

योऽन्तःसुखोऽन्तरारामस्तथान्तर्ज्योतिरेव यः ।
yo'ntaḥsukho'ntarārāmastathāntarjyotireva yaḥ
स योगी ब्रह्मनिर्वाणं ब्रह्मभूतोऽधिगच्छति ॥५-२४॥
sa yogī brahmanirvāṇaṁ brahmabhūto'dhigacchati (5-24)

— ॐ —

योऽन्तःसुखोऽन्तरारामस्तथान्तर्ज्योतिरेव यः ।
yo'ntaḥsukho'ntarārāmastathāntarjyotireva yaḥ
स योगी ब्रह्मनिर्वाणं ब्रह्मभूतोऽधिगच्छति ॥५-२४॥
sa yogī brahmanirvāṇaṁ brahmabhūto'dhigacchati (5-24)

ॐ तत्सदिति श्रीमद्भगवद्गीतासूपनिषत्सु ब्रह्मविद्यायां योगशास्त्रे श्रीकृष्णार्जुनसंवादे
om tatsaditi śrīmadbhagavadgītāsūpaniṣatsu brahmavidyāyāṁ yogaśāstre śrīkṛṣṇārjunasaṁvāde
संन्यासयोगो नाम पञ्चमोऽध्यायः श्लोकः २४
saṁnyāsayogo nāma pañcamo'dhyāyaḥ ślokaḥ 24

Om-Tat-Sat—Om (Braham) is the sole Reality. In the Yogic Scripture on the Science-of-Braham, the Shrimada-Bhāgvada-Gītā Upanishad, we hereby conclude Shloka 24 of the Dialogue between Shrī Krishna and Arjuna entitled Sanyāsa-Yoga, Canto V.

— ॐ सप्ततल प्रभेत्त्रे नमः ॐ —

The Cool Moon of Serenity Rises with the Quelling of Desires

The Karma-Yogi lives in calm, like the moonlight aglow,
Not touched by delight, nor weighed down by sorrow.
He neither runs away, nor chases—
He knows the worldly dream appears sparkling bright,
but is fake for it stays infinitely brief.
When passions melt and sorrows wane into the mist,
then alone the soul stays like the Stainless Infinite.

— o —

O heart, let these fevered flames be stilled,
With neither loss nor triumph should thy mind stay filled.
Then alone shalt thou shine, serene in tranquil light,
A mirrored lake clear, poised for the silent Infinite

— o —

Lo, look at the Karma-Yogi.

He did not gather. He only remembered.
He did not journey. Yet he arrived.
And at there—within that still blaze—he became merged;
Not vanished, but fulfilled.

— o —

Illumined with the inner light.

Content within the Self; partaking the joy of the Self—
The Yogi attained mergence in Braham: who is all bliss.

— o —

He had asked for nothing, and thus he received all—
Obtained not from the world, but from his within Self.
He now drinks from the infinite well no hand can draw,
no thirst exhaust.

— o —

Nay, nay—he's not dry, but verily bliss personified.

He does rejoice—not in others or objects, but in his own beingness.
He dwells not in motions—but in Knowingness,
Not in speech—but in Silence,
And with a tranquil silence always singing within his self.

ॐ गीता श्लोकः ५.२५ – GĪTĀ VERSE 5.25

ॐ श्रीमद्भगवद्गीतासूपनिषत्सु ब्रह्मविद्यायां योगशास्त्रे श्रीकृष्णार्जुनसंवादे
om śrīmadbhagavadgītāsūpaniṣatsu brahmavidyāyāṁ yogaśāstre śrīkṛṣṇārjunasaṁvāde
संन्यासयोगो नाम पञ्चमोऽध्यायः श्लोकः २५
saṁnyāsayogo nāma pañcamo'dhyāyaḥ ślokaḥ 25

— ॐ —

लभन्ते ब्रह्मनिर्वाणमृषयः क्षीणकल्मषाः ।
labhante brahmanirvāṇamṛṣayaḥ kṣīṇakalmaṣāḥ
छिन्नद्वैधा यतात्मानः सर्वभूतहिते रताः ॥५-२५॥
chinnadvaidhā yatātmānaḥ sarvabhūtahite ratāḥ (5-25)

The sage whose sins have been purged, whose doubts have been dispelled, whose disciplined mind is firmly established in the Lord, who persists devoted to the welfare of all beings—attains to Brahama: the ocean of bliss. (5.25)

—: Word-by-Word :—

लभन्ते labhante – attain; ब्रह्मनिर्वाणम् brahma-nirvāṇam – liberation in Brahman; ऋषयः ṛṣayaḥ – the sages; क्षीणकल्मषाः kṣīṇa-kalmaṣāḥ – whose impurities are destroyed; छिन्नद्वैधाः chinna-dvaidhāḥ – free from dualities; यतात्मानः yatātmānaḥ – self-controlled; सर्वभूतहिते sarva-bhūta-hite – devoted to the welfare of all beings; रताः ratāḥ – engaged.

—: Understanding The Verse :—

— ॐ श्रीकृष्णाय नमः ॐ —

In this beautiful verse, Bhagwāna Shri Krishna extols the inner and outer qualities of those sages (ṛṣayaḥ or śiṣyaḥ) who have attained Brahma-nirvāṇa—the liberation that arises from the realization of Braham.

These exalted beings are not mere thinkers or recluses, but are knowers of Truth, whose lives radiate both purity and universal compassion.

The verse identifies several hallmarks of their realization:
- the eradication of past karmic impurities क्षीणकल्मषाः (kṣīṇa-kalmaṣāḥ),
- the dissolution of doubt छिन्नद्वैधा (chinna-dvaidhāḥ),
- the steady discipline of the inner being यतात्मानः (yatātmānaḥ),
- and the all-encompassing love expressed through unceasing dedication to the welfare of all beings सर्वभूतहिते रताः (sarva-bhūta-hite ratāḥ).

— ॐ श्रीरामाय नमः ॐ —

These are not qualities that develop in isolation.

Rather, they are the fruit of sustained साधना sādhanā, philosophical inquiry, renunciation, and deep inner absorption—likely over many human lives.

Such sages attain Braham, who is शन्तिः परमं śāntim paramām—Supreme Peace—the ultimate goal of human existence.

—: Key Sanskrit Terms :—

Let us lift the Sanskrit words like small lamps in the dusk, watching how their quiet light gathers the shadows, shapes them, softens them, and shows us what hitherto lay hidden.

— ॐ —

लभन्ते ब्रह्मनिर्वाणम् ऋषयः (Labhante brahmanirvāṇam ṛṣayaḥ):
- ऋषयः ṛṣayaḥ — the seers, those of purified vision
- लभन्ते labhante — attain
- ब्रह्मनिर्वाणम् brahmanirvāṇam — absorption into Braham, the state of undisturbed bliss and infinite being.

The ऋषि ṛṣi is not merely a knower of scriptures but a knower of the Self.

— ॐ —

क्षीणकल्मषाः (Kṣīṇakalmaṣāḥ):
- Their कल्मषाः kalmaṣa — the stains of ignorance and sin
- are क्षीण kṣīṇa — completely worn away.

Their hearts, purified by knowledge, devotion, and ordained-karma, have become stainless, like clear waters reflecting the sun.

— ॐ —

छिन्नद्वैधाः (Chinnadvaidhāḥ):
-Their द्वैधाः dvaidha — the inner split caused by doubt, desire, and delusion
- has been छिन्न chinna — cut asunder.

No longer are they torn between opposing currents; their consciousness is unified, whole, unwavering.

— ॐ —

यतात्मानः (Yatātmānaḥ):
- They are यतात्मानः yatātmānaḥ — masters of themselves.

The senses and mind, once turbulent, are now fully disciplined and peaceful, harnessed under the rule of the illumined Self.

— ॐ —

सर्वभूतहिते रताः (Sarvabhūtahite ratāḥ):
-They rejoice रताः (ratāḥ) in
- सर्वभूतहिते sarvabhūtahita — the welfare of all beings.

Their realization is not a dry withdrawal, but a flowering of spontaneous compassion, for they see their own Self shining in everything in existence.

This verse beautifully unveils the portrait of the perfected sage: pure, unified, disciplined, and overflowing with universal goodwill.

—: In Brief :—

— ॐ श्रीकृष्णाय नमः ॐ —

In this verse, Shri Krishna offers a vision of the realized sage, the one who has transcended the entanglements of काम kāma (desire), क्रोध krodha (anger), अहंकार ahaṅkāra (ego), and अविद्या avidyā (ignorance), and has become a vessel of truth, compassion, and liberation.

The phrase "क्षीणकल्मषाः kṣīṇa-kalmaṣāḥ" denotes those whose sins and impurities have been washed away—not just gross misdeeds, but the subtle residues of karma, the deep-rooted tendencies वासना (vāsanās) that drive attachment, aversion, and bondage. These are removed through the fire of Self-knowledge, which leaves the heart pure and undivided.

"छिन्नद्वैधा Chinna-dvaidhāḥ"—the doubts that arise from ignorance, the mental indecision that clouds discernment, have been cut asunder.

Doubt does not merely refer to uncertainty in thought, but to the existential confusion about who we are, what is real, and what is eternal. With the realization of Braham, this division is healed. The seeker no longer sees himself as separate from others, or from the Whole.

— ॐ श्रीरामाय नमः ॐ —

The term "यतात्मानः yatātmānaḥ" refers to those whose inner faculties—mind, intellect, and senses—have been disciplined and harmonized.

Such a one no longer acts from impulse, but from clarity and stillness. The Self has become the master, and the instruments of perception and action follow its silent command.

— ॐ त्रिलोकेश्वराय नमः ॐ —

Crucially, the sage is "सर्वभूतहिते रताः sarva-bhūta-hite ratāḥ"—one who delights in the welfare of all; aye all beings—not necessarily just other humans for all beings are the expressions of Braham.

This universal goodwill is not a cultivated moral duty but a natural expression of realized oneness. Having seen the Self in all beings and all beings in the Self, the sage's compassion is inclusive, unconditional, and effortless. He does not serve others to gain merit or praise, but because he no longer sees any real separation between himself and others.

Such beings are said to attain "ब्रह्मनिर्वाणम् brahma-nirvāṇam"—the quiescence of all individuality into Braham, which is described elsewhere as "शान्तिः पराम śāntiḥ parām"—the supreme peace that is not a state of mental quiet, but the very essence of Braham Itself.

This is liberation while living (जीवन-मुक्ति jīvanmukti), where the sage, though still appearing in a body, rests inwardly in the eternal, changeless, blissful Self.

— ॐ लीलामाणिक्याय नमः ॐ —

This verse affirms the fruit of Self-realization: not merely an inward absorption, but also an outward flowering of love, wisdom, and peace. The sage becomes a living embodiment of Braham, and a silent benefactor of all creation.

In the next verse, Shri Krishna will go on to describe the direct experience of Braham by such liberated beings—showing how their union with the Supreme is both complete and irreversible.

— ॐ तत सत ॐ —

Before moving on, let us once more bow in deep reverence before this sacred verse of the Bhagavad-Gītā, an eternal beacon of wisdom that ceaselessly illumines the path of seekers. Engage with its form—inscribe it with your own hand, let your heart dwell upon its meaning, and raise your voice in its chanting—for within these syllables echoes the undying proclamation delivered millennia ago on the battlefield of Kurukshetra. These words, transmitted unchanged across the unbroken chain of generations, form a living bridge, linking us to that sanctified era when Bhagwāna Shri Krishna Himself walked this earth and bestowed this divine teaching. Through the luminous vibration of these sacred Sanskrit sounds, we are drawn nearer to His timeless presence, touching the very heartbeat of the Eternal.

— ॐ —

लभन्ते ब्रह्मनिर्वाणमृषयः क्षीणकल्मषाः ।
labhante brahmanirvāṇamṛṣayaḥ kṣīṇakalmaṣāḥ
छिन्नद्वैधा यतात्मानः सर्वभूतहिते रताः ॥५-२५॥
chinnadvaidhā yatātmānaḥ sarvabhūtahite ratāḥ (5-25)

लभन्ते ब्रह्मनिर्वाणमृषयः क्षीणकल्मषाः ।
labhante brahmanirvāṇamṛṣayaḥ kṣīṇakalmaṣāḥ
छिन्नद्वैधा यतात्मानः सर्वभूतहिते रताः ॥५-२५॥
chinnadvaidhā yatātmānaḥ sarvabhūtahite ratāḥ (5-25)

ॐ तत्सदिति श्रीमद्भगवद्गीतासूपनिषत्सु ब्रह्मविद्यायां योगशास्त्रे श्रीकृष्णार्जुनसंवादे
om tatsaditi śrīmadbhagavadgītāsūpaniṣatsu brahmavidyāyāṁ yogaśāstre śrīkṛṣṇārjunasaṁvāde
संन्यासयोगो नाम पञ्चमोऽध्यायः श्लोकः २५
saṁnyāsayogo nāma pañcamo'dhyāyaḥ ślokaḥ 25

Om-Tat-Sat—Om (Braham) is the sole Reality. In the Yogic Scripture on the Science-of-Braham, the Shrimada-Bhāgvada-Gītā Upanishad, we hereby conclude Shloka 25 of the Dialogue between Shrī Krishna and Arjuna entitled Sanyāsa-Yoga, Canto V.

O Pilgrim Know:

Where dust of praise, nor ash of blame can stay,
No wave of birth, no tide of death—nor night, nor day,
Exits a shore unseen which our ancient Rishis didst see,
Following a radiant way — to an unmeasured Sea-of-Bliss.

—o—

It's a path not for those seeking wreaths of gold,
Nor who huddle amid hordes, or stay seated on thrones of words—
But they who have walked through heat of their own soul's fire.
And now dwell in peace—all doubts gone—like mist dissolved at dawn,
Sins winnowed—like leaves swept away in autumnal storm.

—o—

Past flowers & dirt blowing on the road,
Past fading voices—with Praise dissolving in same thin air as Blame,
In the silence between two breaths,
Behold—for someone is coming through.
Past streets, and fields, and the bargaining cries of bazaars—
he moves through the world—as streaks of golden-sparks.

—o—

Nay, not a seeker of gold, nor a scribe sitting in some narrow cell—
This one is different,
—For he once burned in a fire-without-smoke until nothing remained:
Except what did remain: A deep clear lake and a windless hymn.

—o—

O behold: for the Yogi has set himself down—
Now he's like a garment resting by the river's edge,
—And lo, the river is folding him into its mouth to becomes the Sea—
A sea called satt-chitt-ānanda braham:
the seamless ocean of consciousness without shores.

—o—

O mortal: One day, do thou too be like that Rishi of yore,
Of whom Krishna Himself speaks of in verse Five-twenty-five (5.25).

ॐ गीता श्लोकः ५.२६ – GĪTĀ VERSE 5.26

ॐ श्रीमद्भगवद्गीतासूपनिषत्सु ब्रह्मविद्यायां योगशास्त्रे श्रीकृष्णार्जुनसंवादे
om śrīmadbhagavadgītāsūpaniṣatsu brahmavidyāyāṁ yogaśāstre śrīkṛṣṇārjunasaṁvāde
संन्यासयोगो नाम पञ्चमोऽध्यायः श्लोकः २६
saṁnyāsayogo nāma pañcamo'dhyāyaḥ ślokaḥ 26

— ॐ —

कामक्रोधवियुक्तानां यतीनां यतचेतसाम् ।
kāmakrodhaviyuktānāṁ yatīnāṁ yatacetasām
अभितो ब्रह्मनिर्वाणं वर्तते विदितात्मनाम् ॥५-२६॥
abhito brahmanirvāṇaṁ vartate viditātmanām (5-26)

The sage who is free of desire and ire, who has subdued his mind, who has realized the Self, verily attains Nirvāna—a forever mergence in Brahama, the all-pervading existence replete with bliss and consciousness. (5.26)

—: Word-by-Word :—

कामक्रोधवियुक्तानाम् kāma-krodha-viyuktānām – of those who are free from desire and anger; यतीनाम् yatīnām – of the self-restrained; यतचेतसाम् yata-cetasām – of those with controlled minds; अभितः abhitah – on all sides; ब्रह्मनिर्वाणम् brahma-nirvāṇam – liberation in Brahman; वर्तते vartate – exists; विदितात्मनाम् viditātmanām – of those who have realized the Self.

—: Understanding The Verse :—

— ॐ श्रीकृष्णाय नमः ॐ —

In this verse, Bhagwāna Shri Krishna describes the final spiritual state attained by those who have subdued desire and anger, who have achieved inner mastery, and who have realized the Self.

These are the wise ascetics—not necessarily those who have renounced the world externally, but those who have renounced inwardly, having turned away from the snares of attachment, agitation, and ego.

— ॐ श्रीरामाय नमः ॐ —

Such individuals are pointed to here as "यतयः yatayaḥ"—the self-controlled ones, who through the practice of Sāṅkhya-yoga or contemplative knowledge, have calmed the mind and directed it steadily toward the Supreme.

Their realization is not fragmentary or intellectual, but total and abiding. They live in constant awareness of Braham, the all-pervading, ever-blissful, conscious Reality.

The fruit of their striving is ब्रह्मनिर्वाण Brahma-nirvāṇa—the highest peace, which is not the cessation of existence, but the fullness of Being in which individuality dissolves into the Infinite.

—: *Key Sanskrit Terms* :—

Let us read with the soul as much as the mind. Let the Sanskrit roll through us like wind through reeds—not to carry us away, but to make us still.

— ॐ —

कामक्रोधवियुक्तानां (Kāmakrodhaviyuktānām):
- Those who are वियुक्त viyukta — completely freed
- from काम kāma (desire) and
- क्रोध krodha (anger).

Desire binds the soul outward; anger disrupts inner peace. Freedom from both indicates a mind purified, a heart made tranquil.

— ॐ —

यतीनां यतचेतसाम् (Yatīnām yatacetasām):
The यतीनां yatīnāṁ — the steadfast ascetics, inward renouncers
- whose चेतस् cetas (mind) is
- यत yata (well-controlled).

Such beings are not driven by passion or impulse; their mind has become their servant, not their master.

— ॐ —

विदितात्मनाम् (Viditātmanām):
Those who have विदित आत्मनाम् vidita-ātmanām — who have realized the Self.

It is not bookish knowledge but direct, luminous perception: "I am not this body, this mind, but the eternal, blissful Self."

— ॐ —

अभितः ब्रह्मनिर्वाणं वर्तते (Abhitaḥ brahmanirvāṇaṁ vartate):
- For such souls, ब्रह्मनिर्वाण brahmanirvāṇa — the supreme absorption into Braham
- अभितः वर्तते abhitaḥ vartate — is near, is imminent, surrounds them.

Liberation is not distant, but immediate, like the air enveloping a mountain summit.

This grand verse brings forth the grandeur of the sage's inner conquest—revealing the serene approach to the Infinite. Free from desire and anger, disciplined, they realize Braham and they partake of bliss.

Let us read the verse once again—for each syllable quiets the heart into evening calm, with the wind stilled at dusk.

—: In Brief :—

— ॐ श्रीकृष्णाय नमः ॐ —

Shri Krishna here praises the supreme attainment of the wise, describing them as "कामक्रोधवियुक्तानां ... kāma-krodha-viyuktānām..."—those who have severed all ties with desire and anger, who have mastered the mind, and live in unbroken awareness of the Self.

Desire काम (kāma) and anger क्रोध (krodha) are the two most formidable obstacles to inner peace. The one binds with longing, and the other agitates with opposition. Together they disturb the mind, cloud discernment, and perpetuate bondage. The one who has become free from them is no longer driven by compulsive reaction or craving—he is free.

Such a person is called a यती Yatī—a disciplined renunciant. But renunciation here is not necessarily external; it is inner renunciation of mental modifications, of identification with passions, and of the subtle clinging to the ego.

The यती yatī lives not in indifference, but in lucid detachment—his mind चेतस् (cetas) is यत (yata), restrained, still, and luminous.

— ॐ श्रीरामाय नमः ॐ —

The fruit of such realization is "ब्रह्मनिर्वाणं brahma-nirvāṇam"—union with Braham: who is सर्वत्र स्तिथम् sarvatra-sthitam—present everywhere, the substratum of all.

Braham is not confined to a sacred place, a holy scripture, or a fleeting experience. It is the one all-pervading Reality, equally present within and without, above and below, in all beings and beyond all beings.

— ॐ यज्ञफलप्रदाय नमः ॐ —

This realization is not mystical abstraction, but direct perception: to see Braham alone as Real, and all else as its appearance.

For such a sage, the distinction between - the knower, - the known, - and the process of knowing—dissolves into a oneness. He abides in Braham, not as an object of contemplation, but as his very Self.

This state is निर्वाण nirvāṇa, not in the sense of extinction of life or annihilation, but in the sense of extinction of ignorance, agitation, and ego, leaving only peace without end, joy without cause, and consciousness without duality.

— ॐ कपिसैन्यपराक्रमाय नमः ॐ —

To dwell in Braham is to abide in truth, fullness, and freedom. It is मोक्ष mokṣa, the liberation that ends the cycle of becoming. Even while in the body, such a person is untouched by birth and death. He lives as a witness, as a light unto the world, effortless, pure, and serene.

This verse forms a culmination of the path outlined in the chapter: having renounced the fruits of action, disciplined the senses, dissolved egoism, and realized the Self, the seeker becomes the very Braham he had sought.

The verse that follow will proceed to describe the inner method—ध्यान-योग Dhyāna-Yoga—through which such absorption is attained.

— ॐ तत सत ॐ —

Before we move on, let us bow in reverence to this sacred verse. Write it by hand, reflect on its meaning, chant it aloud, make it your own.

— ॐ —

कामक्रोधवियुक्तानां यतीनां यतचेतसाम् ।
kāmakrodhaviyuktānāṁ yatīnāṁ yatacetasām
अभितो ब्रह्मनिर्वाणं वर्तते विदितात्मनाम् ॥५-२६॥
abhito brahmanirvāṇaṁ vartate viditātmanām (5-26)

— ॐ —

कामक्रोधवियुक्तानां यतीनां यतचेतसाम् ।
kāmakrodhaviyuktānāṁ yatīnāṁ yatacetasām
अभितो ब्रह्मनिर्वाणं वर्तते विदितात्मनाम् ॥५-२६॥
abhito brahmanirvāṇaṁ vartate viditātmanām (5-26)

ॐ तत्सदिति श्रीमद्भगवद्गीतासूपनिषत्सु ब्रह्मविद्यायां योगशास्त्रे श्रीकृष्णार्जुनसंवादे
om tatsaditi śrīmadbhagavadgītāsūpaniṣatsu brahmavidyāyāṁ yogaśāstre śrīkṛṣṇārjunasaṁvāde
संन्यासयोगो नाम पञ्चमोऽध्यायः श्लोकः २६
saṁnyāsayogo nāma pañcamo'dhyāyaḥ ślokaḥ 26

Om-Tat-Sat—Om (Braham) is the sole Reality. In the Yogic Scripture on the Science-of-Braham, the Shrimada-Bhāgvada-Gītā Upanishad, we hereby conclude Shloka 26 of the Dialogue between Shrī Krishna and Arjuna entitled Sanyāsa-Yoga, Canto V.

ॐ गीता श्लोकः ५.२७-२८ – Gītā Verse 5.27-28

ॐ श्रीमद्भगवद्गीतासूपनिषत्सु ब्रह्मविद्यायां योगशास्त्रे श्रीकृष्णार्जुनसंवादे
om śrīmadbhagavadgītāsūpaniṣatsu brahmavidyāyāṁ yogaśāstre śrīkṛṣṇārjunasaṁvāde
संन्यासयोगो नाम पञ्चमोऽध्यायः श्लोकः २७-२८
saṁnyāsayogo nāma pañcamo'dhyāyaḥ ślokaḥ 27-28

— ॐ —

स्पर्शान्कृत्वा बहिर्बाह्यांश्चक्षुश्चैवान्तरे भ्रुवोः ।
sparśānkṛtvā bahirbāhyāṁścakṣuścaivāntare bhruvoḥ
प्राणापानौ समौ कृत्वा नासाभ्यन्तरचारिणौ ॥५-२७॥
prāṇāpānau samau kṛtvā nāsābhyantaracāriṇau (5-27)

यतेन्द्रियमनोबुद्धिर्मुनिर्मोक्षपरायणः ।
yatendriyamanobuddhirmunirmokṣaparāyaṇaḥ
विगतेच्छाभयक्रोधो यः सदा मुक्त एव सः ॥५-२८॥
vigatecchābhayakrodho yaḥ sadā mukta eva saḥ (5-28)

Shutting out the external sense-objects; with the gaze fixed upon the space between the eye-brows; regulating the outgoing and incoming breaths moving through the nostrils; with the senses, mind and intellect well restrained; free of fear, ire, desire—the contemplative sage, who has freedom alone as his highest goal, becomes indeed ever free. (5.27-5.28)

—: Word-by-Word :—

स्पर्शान् sparśān – external contacts; कृत्वा bahir – keeping outside; बाह्यान् bāhyān – external; चक्षुः cakṣuḥ – eyes; च eva – and; अन्तरे antare – between; भ्रुवोः bhruvoḥ – the brows; प्राणापानौ prāṇa-apānau – the outgoing and incoming breaths; समौ kṛtvā – making equal; नासाभ्यन्तरचारिणौ nāsā-abhyantara-cāriṇau – moving within the nostrils.

यत-इन्द्रिय-मनो-बुद्धिः yatendriya-mano-buddhiḥ – one who has controlled the senses, mind, and intellect; मुनिः muniḥ – the sage; मोक्ष-परायणः mokṣa-parāyaṇaḥ – intent on liberation; विगत-इच्छा-भय-क्रोधः vigatecchā-bhaya-krodhaḥ – free from desire, fear, and anger; यः yaḥ – who; सदा sadā – always; मुक्तः muktaḥ – liberated; एव eva – indeed; सः saḥ – he.

—: Understanding The Verse :—

— ॐ श्रीकृष्णाय नमः ॐ —

In these two verses, Bhagwāna Shri Krishna offers a succinct and sacred description of ध्यान-योग Dhyāna-Yoga—the Yoga of deep meditation—as the culminating discipline for the realization of the

Supreme Self. Having spoken of the inner state of the liberated sage in the preceding verses, Krishna now outlines the method by which such liberation may be attained.

Here, the physical, mental, and spiritual aspects of meditation are brought together into a single, integrated path. The aspirant is instructed to:

- Withdraw from external sensory distractions (बाह्य-स्पर्शान् bāhya-sparśān)
- Fix the gaze between the eyebrows (भ्रूमध्य bhrū-madhya)
- Regulate the life-breath (प्राणापानौ prāṇa and apāna)
- Restrain the faculties of body, mind, and intellect
- And finally, to dissolve desire, fear, and anger

Such a seeker—steadfast in the vision of मोक्ष mokṣa as the supreme goal—attains to liberation even while living.

These verses mark the transition from philosophy into concrete spiritual practice, thereby bridging knowledge (jñāna), action (karma), and meditation (dhyāna).

—: Key Sanskrit Terms :—

Let us behold the verse as one might gaze upon an ancient fresco, its Sanskrit brushstrokes faded yet full of breath, still whispering their secrets to the steadfast heart.

— ॐ —

स्पर्शान्कृत्वा बहिर्बाह्यान् (Sparśān kṛtvā bahirbāhyān):
- The sage places the स्पर्शा sparśāḥ — sense-contacts
- बहिर्बाह्यान् bahirbāhyān — outside himself.

That is, he withdraws the senses from external objects, recognizing them as outward and transient, unworthy of the inner quest.

— ॐ —

चक्षुः च एव अन्तरे भ्रुवोः (Cakṣuḥ caiva antare bhruvoḥ):
- The gaze चक्षुः (cakṣuḥ) is turned inward, focused
- अन्तरे भ्रुवोः antare bhruvoḥ — between the eyebrows.

This signifies a withdrawal from sensory distractions and an intense inward concentration, the awakening of the inner eye:
- दिव्य चक्षु (divya-cakṣuḥ).

— ॐ —

प्राणापानौ समौ कृत्वा (Prāṇāpānau samau kṛtvā):
- Balancing समौ (samau) the vital forces of
- प्राण prāṇa (outgoing breath) and

- अपान apāna (incoming breath) — a subtle regulation of life-energy to quieten the body and still the mind, drawing
- प्राण prāṇic currents inward toward the center of being.

— ॐ —

यतेन्द्रियमनोबुद्धिः (Yatendriyamanobuddhiḥ):
- One who has restrained यत (yata) the
- इन्द्रिय indriyas (senses),
- मनस् manas (mind), and
- बुद्धि buddhi (intellect).

No longer scattered outwardly, his inner faculties are harmonized and concentrated like a lamp protected from winds.

— ॐ —

मुनिः मोक्षपरायणः (Muniḥ mokṣaparāyaṇaḥ):
-The मुनि muni — the silent, contemplative sage
- has मोक्ष mokṣa (liberation) as his
- sole goal: परायण (parāyaṇa).

All his energies, aspirations, and attentions are drawn toward the supreme freedom.

— ॐ —

विगत-इच्छा-भय-क्रोधः (Vigata-icchā-bhaya-krodhaḥ):
- विगत Free from इच्छा icchā (desire),
- भय bhaya (fear), and
- क्रोध krodha (anger)

— the three knots that bind the soul to संसार saṁsāra. Their absence signals complete inner stillness and fearlessness.

— ॐ —

सदा मुक्तः एव सः (Sadā muktaḥ eva saḥ):

Such a sage is सदा मुक्तः sadā muktaḥ — ever free, not intermittently but permanently, established in unbroken liberation.

Lo, see how beautifully each phrase here reveals the method and the luminous fruit of profound meditation and Self-absorption. O behold the yogi sitting unmoved—senses restrained, gaze steady between brows, breath balanced, mind pacified. Each word shapes the form of discipline that flowers into peace, the whole being offered like incense unto the Eternal.

—: In Brief :—

These verses paint the portrait of a meditative sage मुनि (muni), whose entire being is consecrated to मोक्ष mokṣa, to absolute liberation. The method of practice described here is not mechanical but sacred, grounded in deep dispassion, discipline, and devotion.

The aspirant is said to "shut out the external sense-objects" (स्पर्शान्कृत्वा बहि बाह्यान् sparśān kṛtvā bahi bāhyān). This is not merely a physical withdrawal but an inward turning of consciousness.

The senses are no longer scattered upon the world, but gathered and restrained, not by suppression, but through वैराग्य vairāgya, the deep recognition that sense-objects are transient and incapable of yielding lasting joy.

— ॐ श्रीरामाय नमः ॐ —

The fixing of the gaze between the eyebrows भ्रुवोः अन्तरे bhruvoḥ antare (or मध्य madhye) is an ancient practice taught in Yoga. It is not just physiological—it is symbolic of one-pointed concentration एकाग्रता (ekāgratā).

This location corresponds to the आज्ञा चक्र ājnā-chakra, the seat of higher perception. It is here that the mind becomes luminous, and the lower mental waves are transcended.

— ॐ आर्याय नमः ॐ —

Breath regulation (प्राणापानौ समौ कृत्वा prāṇāpānau samau kṛtvā nāsābhyantara-cāriṇau) follows naturally.

- The flow of breath—usually turbulent, uneven, and linked to mental fluctuation—is harmonized.
- When breath becomes gentle, even, and silent, the mind too becomes still.

This balance of प्राणापानौ prāṇa and apāna, especially through सुसुम्ना नाडी suṣumnā-nāḍī, awakens the deeper faculties of awareness.

— ॐ सर्वविगुणवर्जिताय नमः ॐ —

The next stage is restraint of the senses, the mind, and the intellect (इन्द्रिय-मनो-बुद्धि indriya-mano-buddhi).

The sage here is not one who merely suppresses thought but one whose faculties have been purified, trained, and surrendered to the Self. The will is sovereign, the intellect unwavering, and the heart serene.

— ॐ जैत्राय नमः ॐ —

In such a state, काम क्रोध भय kāma, krodha, and bhaya—desire, anger, and fear—are said to have departed विगत (vigata).

These three are the principal inner enemies of peace. Desire clings to the future, anger reacts to the past, and fear trembles in the present. Their cessation signals the stillness of the ego and the rise of the Self.

Such a sage is a true मुनि muni—a contemplative one who, मोक्ष परायण mokṣa-parāyaṇaḥ, has liberation as his sole aim and inner refuge.

He does not seek heaven, nor power, nor pleasure, but the Supreme Abode परम-धाम (parama-dhāma), the Braham that is beyond all limitation, where sorrow cannot enter and joy does not wane.

— ॐ द्वारकानाथाय नमः ॐ —

The use of एव eva ("indeed" or "alone") throughout these verses emphasizes the certainty and exclusiveness of this path.

It is not one path among many, but the culmination of all disciplines—knowledge, devotion, ordained-karma—merging into meditative absorption in the Self.

In this sacred state, even as the breath flows gently and thought ceases, the aspirant becomes free—ever free विमुक्तः (vimuktaḥ).

No longer bound by body, role, or memory, he abides as pure awareness, as peace itself, as Braham.

— ॐ महादेवाय नमः ॐ —

Thus, through the path of ध्यान-योग Dhyāna-Yoga, Bhagwāna Shri Krishna shows how the restless soul is calmed, and how the seeker, step by step, becomes the very Goal he once sought.

The next verse will close the chapter by declaring the Supreme Lord—who is the manifest form of Bhagwāna Shri Krishna and not merely the formless Braham—to be the ultimate refuge, the culmination of all paths, thereby uniting the wisdom of Vedānta with the grace of devotion (bhakti).

— ॐ तत सत ॐ —

Before we move on, let us bow in reverence to this sacred verse. Write it by hand, reflect on its meaning, chant it aloud, make it your own.

— ॐ —

स्पर्शान्कृत्वा बहिर्बाह्यांश्चक्षुश्चैवान्तरे भ्रुवोः ।
sparśānkṛtvā bahirbāhyāṁścakṣuścaivāntare bhruvoḥ
प्राणापानौ समौ कृत्वा नासाभ्यन्तरचारिणौ ॥५-२७॥
prāṇāpānau samau kṛtvā nāsābhyantaracāriṇau (5-27)

यतेन्द्रियमनोबुद्धिर्मुनिर्मोक्षपरायणः ।
yatendriyamanobuddhirmunirmokṣaparāyaṇaḥ
विगतेच्छाभयक्रोधो यः सदा मुक्त एव सः ॥५-२८॥
vigatecchābhayakrodho yaḥ sadā mukta eva saḥ (5-28)

—ॐ—

स्पर्शान्कृत्वा बहिर्बाह्यांश्चक्षुश्चैवान्तरे भ्रुवोः ।
sparśānkṛtvā bahirbāhyāmścakṣuścaivāntare bhruvoḥ
प्राणापानौ समौ कृत्वा नासाभ्यन्तरचारिणौ ॥५-२७॥
prāṇāpānau samau kṛtvā nāsābhyantaracāriṇau (5-27)
यतेन्द्रियमनोबुद्धिर्मुनिर्मोक्षपरायणः ।
yatendriyamanobuddhirmunirmokṣaparāyaṇaḥ
विगतेच्छाभयक्रोधो यः सदा मुक्त एव सः ॥५-२८॥
vigatecchābhayakrodho yaḥ sadā mukta eva saḥ (5-28)

ॐ तत्सदिति श्रीमद्भगवद्गीतासूपनिषत्सु ब्रह्मविद्यायां योगशास्त्रे श्रीकृष्णार्जुनसंवादे
om tatsaditi śrīmadbhagavadgītāsūpaniṣatsu brahmavidyāyāṁ yogaśāstre śrīkṛṣṇārjunasaṁvāde
संन्यासयोगो नाम पञ्चमोऽध्यायः श्लोकः २७-२८
saṁnyāsayogo nāma pañcamo'dhyāyaḥ ślokaḥ 27-28

Om-Tat-Sat—Om (Braham) is the sole Reality. In the Yogic Scripture on the Science-of-Braham, the Shrimada-Bhāgvada-Gītā Upanishad, we hereby conclude Shloka 27-28 of the Dialogue between Shrī Krishna and Arjuna entitled Sanyāsa-Yoga, Canto V.

— ॐ योगीश्वराय नमः ॐ —

<u>Ah... Death: the Great Clarifier</u>

O mortal, tarry not. Do not wait. Do not delay. Never put-off.
For the moment of reckoning can come at any time!

Like it or not—but the perfume of youth fades over time.
The garland starts to rot.
Alas. now the mortgage itself expires.
Suddenly the rich mighty man finds himself clutching:
At a rosary with trembling hands.

Though too late and of no avail—and yet he asks:
"What is it that doesn't die?
O please someone, tell me quick—that I am the eternal ātmā."

O fool – now it's too late for thee.
Later perhaps—maybe.
Try next time—when you get another human birth in a thousand years.
Meantime live as the animals you have stayed as—and eaten.

ॐ गीता श्लोकः ५.२९ – GĪTĀ VERSE 5.29

ॐ श्रीमद्भगवद्गीतासूपनिषत्सु ब्रह्मविद्यायां योगशास्त्रे श्रीकृष्णार्जुनसंवादे
om śrīmadbhagavadgītāsūpaniṣatsu brahmavidyāyāṁ yogaśāstre śrīkṛṣṇārjunasaṁvāde
संन्यासयोगो नाम पञ्चमोऽध्यायः श्लोकः २९
saṁnyāsayogo nāma pañcamo'dhyāyaḥ ślokaḥ 29

— ॐ —

भोक्तारं यज्ञतपसां सर्वलोकमहेश्वरम् ।
bhoktāraṁ yajñatapasāṁ sarvalokamaheśvaram
सुहृदं सर्वभूतानां ज्ञात्वा मां शान्तिमृच्छति ॥५-२९॥
suhṛdaṁ sarvabhūtānāṁ jñātvā māṁ śāntimṛcchati (5-29)

Knowing Me—the final partaker of all sacrifices and austerities, the great Lord of the world, the selfless friend of all—My devotee attains abiding peace." (5.29)

—: *Word-by-Word* :—

भोक्तारम् bhoktāram – the enjoyer; यज्ञतपसाम् yajña-tapasām – of sacrifices and austerities; सर्वलोकमहेश्वरम् sarva-loka-maheśvaram – the supreme Lord of all worlds; सुहृदम् suhṛdam – the friend; सर्वभूतानाम् sarva-bhūtānām – of all beings; ज्ञात्वा jñātvā – knowing; माम् mām – me; शान्तिम् śāntim – peace; ऋच्छति ṛcchati – attains.

—: *Understanding The Verse* :—

— ॐ श्रीकृष्णाय नमः ॐ —

In this conclusive verse of the fifth chapter, Bhagwāna Shri Krishna reveals the ultimate truth that underlies all the paths and disciplines previously described.

Krishna affirms that the supreme goal of all sacrifices (yajñas), austerities (tapasyās), and all spiritual undertakings is Himself. Not as an abstract Braham alone, but as the personal Divine—Iśvara, the Supreme Lord, the eternal friend of all beings, and the true object of devotion.

Krishna here declares three supreme aspects of His divine identity:
- Partaker of all यज्ञ yajñas and तप tapas (भोक्तारं यज्ञतपसां bhoktāraṁ yajña-tapasām).
- महा-ईश्वर Mahā-īśvara—the Great-Lord—of all worlds (सर्वलोकमहेश्वरम् sarva-loka-maheśvaram).
- सुहृदं The well-wisher and intimate friend of all beings (सुहृदं सर्वभूतानां suhṛdaṁ sarva-bhūtānām).

— ॐ श्रीरामाय नमः ॐ —

These truths, once fully known and internalized by the devotee, bring about not merely philosophical insight, but abiding and unshakeable peace शान्तिमृच्छति (śāntim ṛcchhati).

This verse thus brings together the disciplines of कर्म ज्ञान भक्ति karma, jñāna, and bhakti into a single realization—knowing and surrendering to the Divine Person who is both immanent and transcendent.

—: Key Sanskrit Terms :—

Turning to the heart of the verse, let us reflect on its words each of which will lead us towards deeper understanding. Let us close with the Sanskrit as with a chant rising to benediction. "The yogi knows Me as the enjoyer of sacrifice, friend of all beings, Lord of the world." Each syllable seals the chapter in companionship and release.

— ॐ —

भोक्तारं यज्ञतपसाम् (Bhoktāraṁ yajñatapasām):
- The Supreme is the भोक्ता bhoktā — the final recipient and enjoyer
- of all यज्ञ yajña (sacrifices) and
- तपस tapas (austerities).

Every act of sacrifice, offering, or penance ultimately reaches Him alone, even if performed with varied intentions.

— ॐ —

सर्वलोकमहेश्वरम् (Sarvalokamaheśvaram):
- He is the महेश्वर maheśvara — the great Lord
- of सर्वलोक sarvaloka — all worlds, all planes of existence.

Not bound to one realm or form, the Divine pervades and transcends all creation, sustaining it in His own Being.

— ॐ —

सुहृदं सर्वभूतानाम् (Suhṛdaṁ sarvabhūtānām):
- The Supreme is the सुहृद suhṛd: true, secret, and selfless Friend
- of all beings सर्वभूतानाम् (sarvabhūtānām).

Unlike worldly friendships tinged with expectation, His friendship is pure, unconditional, and eternally benevolent.

— ॐ —

ज्ञात्वा मां (Jñātvā māṁ):
- ज्ञात्वा Knowing
- मां Me — not merely intellectually, but through direct spiritual realization;

knowing Me thus as the inner Lord, the friend, the final goal — that is the true knowledge which liberates.

— ॐ —

शान्तिम् ऋच्छति (Śāntim ṛcchati):
- ऋच्छति Attaining
- शान्ति śānti — profound peace — not the transient quietude born of outer circumstances, but the deep, unshakable peace that arises from union with the Eternal.

Through each of its terms, this verse reveals the Divine as both the ultimate Goal and the intimate Companion of all beings — and knowing Him thusly, we seekers can attain that perfect bliss.

—: *In Brief* :—

— ॐ श्रीकृष्णाय नमः ॐ —

In this climactic verse, Shri Krishna reveals the living heart of all spiritual disciplines: not mere renunciation, nor abstract knowledge, but the personal recognition and devotion to the Supreme Lord—the one who lovingly accepts all offerings, who rules all worlds with majesty, and who dwells in every heart as the most intimate friend.

— ॐ श्रीरामाय नमः ॐ —

The phrase "भोक्तारं यज्ञतपसां bhoktāraṁ yajña-tapasām" teaches that all sacrifices and austerities—whether Vedic rituals, disciplined fasting, charitable giving, or penance—ultimately reach only Him.

Though outer forms may differ, it is Krishna Himself who is the inner enjoyer, for it is by His presence that all these acts are made meaningful.

When a यज्ञ yajña is offered to a lesser deity, or तपस tapas is performed for personal gain, their fruits are bound by karma. But when these are offered with devotion to Bhagwāna, they become means of liberation.

— ॐ सत्यमूर्तये नमः ॐ —

He is also "सर्वलोकमहेश्वरम् sarva-loka-maheśvaram"—the Great Lord of all the worlds.
This refers not only to His cosmic sovereignty, but also to His lordship over the individual heart, the mind, and the senses.
He is the source and sustainer of all that exists—visible and invisible. This realization removes all pride and anxiety; for what belongs to the Lord cannot truly be claimed by the ego.

— ॐ श्रीकृष्णाय नमः ॐ —

Krishna's lordship is not cold or distant. He is "सुहृदं सर्वभूतानां suhṛdaṁ sarva-bhūtānām"—the well-wishing friend of all beings.

This is one of the most tender revelations of the Gītā.

God is not a judge from afar, nor merely the abstract Absolute.

He is the ever-compassionate companion, desiring the good of all, even of those who deny Him.

He is the friend in joy and sorrow, the silent helper in times of trial, and the inner witness who never abandons the soul, no matter how lost.

— ॐ मेघश्यामाय नमः ॐ —

When a devotee realizes these three aspects—the divine enjoyer, the cosmic Lord, and the intimate friend—his heart is filled not merely with reverence, but with deep, abiding peace.

There is no longer room for fear, for all actions are sanctified; no space for restlessness, for the Lord governs all; no place for loneliness, for God is ever near.

The phrase "ज्ञात्वा मां jñātvā māṁ"—"knowing Me"—is not intellectual. It means recognizing and experiencing Krishna in all three aspects, through loving devotion (bhakti), humility, and surrender.

Such a knower, says the Lord, "शान्तिमृच्छति śāntim ṛcchhati"—attains peace, not temporary tranquility, but permanent liberation—the peace of union with the Divine.

— ॐ दयानिधानाय नमः ॐ —

This final verse of Chapter 5, having expounded the discipline of karma-yoga, meditation, renunciation, and Self-realization, culminates in bhakti—a full-hearted recognition of Krishna as the ultimate refuge, the Lord, and the beloved friend. It prepares the way for the next chapter, where the path of meditative absorption ध्यान-योग (Dhyāna-Yoga) will be detailed more fully.

Thus, the fifth chapter closes not in abstraction but in divine intimacy—offering to the seeker the secret of peace: know the Lord, offer all to Him, and abide in His friendship.

— ॐ तत सत ॐ —

Before we move on, let us bow in reverence to this sacred verse. Write it by hand, reflect on its meaning, chant it aloud, make it your own.

— ॐ —

भोक्तारं यज्ञतपसां सर्वलोकमहेश्वरम् ।
bhoktāraṁ yajñatapasāṁ sarvalokamaheśvaram
सुहृदं सर्वभूतानां ज्ञात्वा मां शान्तिमृच्छति ॥५-२९॥
suhṛdaṁ sarvabhūtānāṁ jñātvā māṁ śāntimṛcchati (5-29)

— ॐ —

भोक्तारं यज्ञतपसां सर्वलोकमहेश्वरम् ।
bhoktāraṁ yajñatapasāṁ sarvalokamaheśvaram
सुहृदं सर्वभूतानां ज्ञात्वा मां शान्तिमृच्छति ॥५-२९॥
suhṛdaṁ sarvabhūtānāṁ jñātvā māṁ śāntimṛcchati (5-29)

ॐ तत्सदिति श्रीमद्भगवद्गीतासूपनिषत्सु ब्रह्मविद्यायां योगशास्त्रे श्रीकृष्णार्जुनसंवादे
om tatsaditi śrīmadbhagavadgītāsūpaniṣatsu brahmavidyāyāṁ yogaśāstre śrīkṛṣṇārjunasaṁvāde
संन्यासयोगो नाम पञ्चमोऽध्यायः श्लोकः २९
saṁnyāsayogo nāma pañcamo'dhyāyaḥ ślokaḥ 29

Om-Tat-Sat—Om (Braham) is the sole Reality. In the Yogic Scripture on the Science-of-Braham, the Shrimada-Bhāgvada-Gītā Upanishad, we hereby conclude Shloka 29 of the Dialogue between Shrī Krishna and Arjuna entitled Sanyāsa-Yoga, Canto V.

— ॐ सत्यव्रताय नमः ॐ —

The Rivers Flow. The Ocean Waits in Stillness
From snow-clad heights and shadowed forest glen,
The rivers run through fields and fates of men.
They leap through stones, and weep through desert air,
Yet all are one day drawn—to the Ocean's final care.
So too, all acts of worship, toil, and flame,
Are offered unto Him—from whom they came.

— o —

One day the seeker reaches That changeless shore,
Then he wanders no more, but rests for evermore.
O behold, for when the waves are gone—just the waveless Depth remains.

— o —

This is all He—Krishna—sporting.
And the one redeeming feature of His Leela is this:
Having known Him—
the great Lord of the world, the selfless friend of all,
the final partaker of all yajnas and karmas—
one day we do reach our Home,
And finally we attain that abiding bliss—
in Him: our Lord-God Bhagwana Shri Krishna.

ॐ CHAPTER FIVE RECAP

— ॐ —

In the esoteric unfolding of the Bhagavad-Gītā, the **Fifth-Canto—Karma-Saṁnyāsa Yoga**—granted us a vision of spiritual harmony: a vision in which renunciation and action, seemingly at odds, were reconciled in the higher light of inner detachment and Self-knowledge. In this luminous discourse of , we were led beyond the surface of outer renunciation into the heart of true saṁnyāsa—the quiet renunciation of ego and desire, even amidst the world of action.

— ॐ —

This canto stands as a luminous summit, bringing together with graceful harmony the paths of renunciation (saṁnyāsa) and selfless action (karma-yoga). What may have seemed distinct—withdrawal from action on the one hand, and the performance of action without attachment on the other—is here shown to be, in essence, a single path when rightly understood and inwardly purified.

— ॐ —

The canto began with Arjuna's earnest question—seeking to know which of the two paths is superior. And the Lord, ever compassionate, clarified with precision and depth: that both lead to the supreme goal; but karma-yoga, when practiced with right vision and inner detachment, is swifter and more accessible for the aspirant still dwelling amidst duties.

We learnt that both karma-yoga and saṁnyāsa, when pursued with right understanding, lead to liberation. We also learnt that the path of karma-yoga—performing without attachments of duties ordained by one's Varna-Āshrama dharma, is far easier, more readily accessible and, when illumined by Jnana, no less exalted.

— ॐ —

Renunciation was shown not as the mere abandonment of karmas, but as the abandonment of clinging and doership. The one who acts for dharma's sake, offering all to the Supreme, stands equal to the one who outwardly renounces.

We were shown the inner stature of the karma-yogin—how he moves through the world untouched, acting without bondage, his heart pure and his mind serene. He sees with clarity that action arises from nature alone; the Self does not act, nor is it stained by action. Thus established in discernment, the wise man rests in peace, even as his body continues its ordained functions.

— ॐ —

We also learnt of the vision of the sage: equal-minded in joy and sorrow, untouched by praise or blame, and even-sighted amidst high and low. He sees all beings with impartial regard, for he perceives the one Self dwelling equally in all. Such vision is not born of intellect alone, but of purified consciousness rooted in the Real.

— ॐ श्रीकृष्णाय नमः ॐ —

Let us now retrace briefly the sacred path we walked through the chapter's verses:

- In the opening, we witnessed Arjuna's inquiry into the relative merits of renunciation and action, and received the Lord's wise answer: that true renunciation lies in freedom from desire, not in forsaking one's duties.
- We then learnt of the karma-yogin—how, through selfless action and inner detachment, he attains peace even while engaged in the world. Such a one, though acting, remains untouched, for his actions are not born of ego.
- The Lord then revealed the mystery of inaction in action—how the wise perceive that the Self does nothing, and that all activity arises from the play of prakṛti alone.
- We were taught that it is ignorance which veils the Divine, and that knowledge alone dispels this delusion. The wise see the Lord as the thread upon which all beings are strung, the indwelling presence in all.
- We beheld the fruits of this wisdom: inner calm, detachment from the senses, freedom from longing, and the unshakable joy of the Self. The sage turns within, rests in the Lord, and dwells in peace.
- Finally, the chapter concluded with the sublime declaration that the Lord is the enjoyer of all offerings, the sovereign of all worlds, and the well-wisher of every being. To know Bhagwāna Shri Krishna thusly is to enter enduring peace.

— ॐ —

Thus, in this chapter we were gently led from duality to unity, from confusion to clarity, from striving to surrender. We learnt that the outer path matters less than the inner orientation. Whether one acts or renounces, it is the relinquishment of craving, the purification of the heart, and the unwavering vision of the Self that lead to freedom.

Having now stood at the confluence of renunciation and action, we find ourselves prepared for the next ascent. In the following chapter, the Lord-God Bhagwāna Shri Krishna shall unveil the way of Dhyāna—the royal path of inward stillness, where the mind is trained to rest in the Self, and the soul is drawn toward the Supreme in silent contemplation.

Aye, the path is long, but each step is illumined for us by Bhagwāna, so let us walk on unwaveringly and with reverence.

ॐ तत्सदिति श्रीमद्भगवद्गीतासूपनिषत्सु ब्रह्मविद्यायां योगशास्त्रे श्रीकृष्णार्जुनसंवादे
om tatsaditi śrīmadbhagavadgītāsūpaniṣatsu brahmavidyāyāṁ yogaśāstre śrīkṛṣṇārjunasaṁvāde
संन्यासयोगो नाम पञ्चमोऽध्यायः ॥
saṁnyāsayogo nāma pañcamo'dhyāyaḥ .

Om-Tat-Sat—Om (Braham) is the sole Reality. In this Yogic Scripture on the Science of Brahama—the Shrimada-Bhāgvada-Gītā Upanishad—hereby ends the dialogue between Shrī Krishna and Arjuna entitled: Sanyāsa Yoga, Canto V.

— ॐ तत सत ॐ —

—o::::oo::::oo::::oo::::oo::::o—

[O Seeker, we thank thee for reading thus far. This has been a brief commentary and lots still remains unsaid. Rāma-willing, our exhaustive commentary will become available by 2027. This is our init endeavor and surely it's full of many faults which we fully own—and we pray thou shalt take it in thy heart to pardon us. Bhagavad-Gita is a celestial stream and any human touch, however well-meaning, only sullies it some. We hope to be forgiven by Bhagwana Shri Krishna for daring to torture this sublime text of His, which has no parallels anywhere—never will.]

ॐ ॐ ॐ ॐ ॐ ॐ ॐ ॐ ॐ ॐ ॐ ॐ ॐ ॐ ॐ ॐ ॐ ॐ

ॐ गीतामाहात्म्यम् GĪTĀ-MĀHĀTMYAM

[Verses on the glory and import of the Bhagavad-Gītā]

— ॐ —

गीताशास्त्रमिदं पुण्यं यः पठेत्प्रयतः पुमान् ।
gītāśāstramidaṁ puṇyaṁ yaḥ paṭhetprayataḥ pumān ,
विष्णोः पदमवाप्नोति भयशोकादिवर्जितः ॥
viṣṇoḥ padamavāpnoti bhayaśokādivarjitaḥ .

One who diligently studies this Bhagavad-Gītā—the bestower of all virtues—with firm devotion and a regulated mind—verily attains Vaikuntha—the holy abode of Māhā-Vishnu—and he stands freed of all the fears and sorrows of this mundane world.

— ॐ —

गीताध्ययनशीलस्य प्राणायामपरस्य च ।
gītādhyayanaśīlasya prāṇāyāmaparasya ca ,
नैव सन्ति हि पापानि पूर्वजन्मकृतानि च ॥
naiva santi hi pāpāni pūrvajanmakṛtāni ca .

One who performs Prāṇāyāms and studies the Bhagavad-Gītā regularly and sincerely—all his sins melt away, even those from all prior lives.

— ॐ —

मलनिर्मोचनं पुंसां जलस्नानं दिने दिने ।
malanirmocanaṁ puṁsāṁ jalasnānaṁ dine dine ,
सकृद्गीताम्भसि स्नानं संसारमलनाशनम् ॥
sakṛdgītāmbhasi snānaṁ saṁsāramalanāśanam .

A daily bath removes external bodily taints, but a single bath in the sacred waters of Bhagavad-Gītā is enough to remove all the taints of this Saṁsāra—this polluting worldly existence of joys, sorrows, births, and deaths.

— ॐ —

गीता सुगीता कर्तव्या किमन्यैः शास्त्रविस्तरैः ।
gītā sugītā kartavyā kimanyaiḥ śāstravistaraiḥ ,
या स्वयं पद्मनाभस्य मुखपद्माद्विनिःसृता ॥
yā svayaṁ padmanābhasya mukhapadmādviniḥsṛtā .

Why go in for other elaborate scriptures, when you can chant the Gītā—the essence of all Vedic scriptures—which issued forth from the lotus mouth of Māhā-Vishnu Himself—on whose navel is the lotus of Creation.

— ॐ —

भारतामृतसर्वस्वं विष्णोर्वक्त्राद्विनिःसृतम् ।
bhāratāmṛtasarvasvaṁ viṣṇorvaktrādviniḥsṛtam ,
गीतागङ्गोदकं पीत्वा पुनर्जन्म न विद्यते ॥
gītāgaṅgodakaṁ pītvā punarjanma na vidyate .

There is no more rebirth for one who partakes of the sacred waters of the Gītā-Gangā—the holy stream which flowed out from the lotus lips of Shri Māhā-Vishnu—the nectar which is the quintessence of Māhā-Bhārata.

— ॐ —

एकं शास्त्रं देवकीपुत्रगीतमेको देवो देवकीपुत्र एव ।
ekaṁ śāstraṁ devakīputragītameko devo devakīputra eva ,
एको मन्त्रस्तस्य नामानि यानि कर्माप्येकं तस्य देवस्य सेवा ॥
eko mantrastasya nāmāni yāni karmāpyekaṁ tasya devasya sevā .

The holy Gītā of Krishna—son of Devakī—is the One Scripture; Krishna—son of Devakī—is the One God; the name Krishna—son of Devakī—is the One Mantra; service to Him—son of Devakī—is the One and only Duty.

ॐ ॐ ॐ ॐ ॐ ॐ ॐ ॐ ॐ ॐ ॐ ॐ ॐ ॐ ॐ ॐ ॐ ॐ

— ॐ —

श्रीकृष्णचरणार्पणमस्तु
śrī kṛṣṇa caraṇāarpaṇamastu
Hereby dedicated to the Lotus Feet of Bhagwāna Shri Krishna.

कायेन वाचा मनसेंद्रियैर्वा । बुद्ध्यात्मना वा प्रकृतिस्वभावात् ।
kāyena vācā manaseṁdriyairvā , buddhyātmanā vā prakritisvabhāvāt ,
करोमि यद्यत् सकलं परस्मै । नारायणायेति समर्पयामि ॥
karomi yadyat sakalaṁ parasmai , nārāyaṇāyeti samarpayāmi .

Whatever it is I do—through body, mind, speech, or sense-organs, or with my intellect and soul, or with my innate natural tendencies—whatever it be—I offer it all unto Narayana (Bhagwāna Shri Krishna / Bhagwāna Shri Rāma).

— ॐ —

या गीता सनातनस्य धर्मस्यामृतरूपिणी ।
yā gītā sanātanasya dharmasyāmṛtarūpiṇī ,
लोकानां मार्गदर्शिनी तस्याः मूलं प्रयच्छामि ॥
lokānāṁ margadarśinī tasyāḥ mūlaṁ prayacchāmi .

That Gītā, which's the nectar-form of Sanātana Dharma—the guide of the worlds upon The-Path—towards Her sacred roots I now proceed to take refuge.

— o —

Ekam-Sanātana-Dharma
एकं सनातन धर्म
Only-True-Religion

Be Inspired and Inspire Others. Light a Lamp of Wisdom.
Start your own Gitā Classes with a Friend Today.